DATE DUE

DEMCO 38-297

Uncertainty and the Labour Market

Uncertainty and the Labour Market:

Recent Developments in Job-Search Theory

C. J. McKENNA
Lecturer in Economics
University College, Cardiff

ST. MARTIN'S PRESS
New York

© C. J. McKenna, 1985

ISBN 0–312–82861–6

Library of Congress Cataloging in Publication Data

McKenna, G.J.
   Uncertainty and the labour market.

   Includes index.
   1. Unemployed — mathematical models. 2. Labor
supply — mathematical models. 3. Job hunting —
mathematical models.
I. Title.
HD5707.M39   1985   331.11   85-1988
ISBN 0–312–82861–6

To Jane

Contents

Preface

In writing this book I have made free use of arguments and suggestions from a variety of friends and colleagues who over the past six years have been kind enough to take an interest in my work. I hope this book reflects the fact that my friends fall into one of two categories: those who insist that detail and a carefully worked structure are essential to an understanding of economics, and those who insist that broader issues and wider implications are always there if you take the trouble to look.

John Hey falls into both categories, which is irksome for my classification but a blessing for his students and the profession. He kindly read the first draft and forced me to rethink Chapter 1. However, his influence may be found in practically every chapter. For his enthusiasm and criticisms, many thanks, and absolution from all blame for remaining errors.

Thanks also to Edward Elgar for his unrestrained encouragement and enthusiasm for this project. Tricia Buckingham, Sandra Simpson and Karen North have, at various times, typed a difficult script with great skill.

The book is dedicated to my wife, Jane, whose work is infinitely more important than mine, though her humour, generosity and kindness will never let her admit it.

Introduction

The idea that individuals might make productive use of unemployed time to search out new job opportunities is not new (see Feinberg, 1978a, and Pissarides, 1976a), for discussions of the antecedents of modern job-search theory). Nor is the idea that markets have fundamentally different characters when exchange prices are not coordinated by an all-knowing market presence, (Arrow, 1959) and when uncertainty about the potential terms of exchange agreements exists.

The initial stimulus to the formal elaboration of the job-search theory was the growth of the literature on the economics of information, of which two papers by Stigler (1961, 1962) are examples, followed by McCall (1965). However, a boost was given to this subject in the late 1960s in the work on the theoretical reappraisal of the Phillips curve relationship — swiftly followed by the apparent breakdown of the empirical relationship itself in the early 1970s.

The period contains some important landmarks in the literature, most notably the volume by Phelps *et al.* (1970) which effectively established the connection between microeconomic decisions and macroeconomic adjustment — the so called 'microfoundations of macroeconomics' (Weintraub, 1977). The job-search theory has been a key element in these 'microfoundations' and the contribution made to the understanding of macroeconomics is studied in Chapter 7 of this book.

It seems fair now to say that the early promise showed by the microfoundations approach soon diminished, partly because of technical complexities involved in forging explicit links between descriptively rich models of individual behaviour and macroeconomic phenomena, but partly also because of the more direct approaches taken by general equilibrium (see Hahn, 1981 for a recent discussion) and developments in macroeconomic modelling — in particular the rational expectations hypothesis (see Begg, 1982).

By this time, however, the job-search theory no longer required continued references to the need for microfoundations in order to justify its existence. The new motivation was the quest for increased generality and increased descriptive richness — the two rarely being achieved simultaneously. It is these developments which occupy us for the first three chapters of the book. Particular attention is given to the structure and solution of the various models, starting with the basic model of sequential search (Chapter 2) and continuing with the various refinements (Chapter 3).

In Chapter 4 the behaviour of the firm is studied along with the market outcome implied by worker and firm interaction in search markets. Students in the field quickly realise that there is little formal analysis of the generation of vacancies or the properties of equilibrium turnover. Although the details of the way *existing* vacancies should be filled by choosing a wage offer or recruitment policy, and the requirements for the existence of 'equilibrium' wage dispersion are well established.

Chapter 5 is a survey of the empirical work on job-search hypotheses available to date. Data problems and econometric difficulties combine to frustrate attempts to translate the rich variety of the theoretical results into distinguishable, testable hypotheses. Chapter 5 studies some of these difficulties, surveys recent attempts to overcome them, and discusses some of the key findings.

Chapters 6 and 7 aim to provide a broader context for job-search theory by studying implications of the analysis for the more familiar areas of microeconomics and macroeconomics. Emphasis is given to the labour supply — consumption decision in the former and to inflation and unemployment theory in the latter.

The book may be read by advanced undergraduates, graduate students and their teachers. Mathematics has been used only where necessary to prepare the reader for some of the analytical tools used in the literature. As far as possible the mathematical solutions are derived in some detail and a full understanding of these does require some knowledge of differential and and integral calculus. The less routine aspects of the mathematics are outlined in three appendices on discounting, conditional expectation and integration by parts.

The help those requiring more than a passing acquaintance with job-search theory the first four chapters are accompanied by exercises. Because of their more discursive nature chapters 6 and 7 are not followed by exercises.

The book's title initially suggests something more general than the analysis of job-search decisions. Two areas of the labour market under uncertainty not studied here are the (static) theory of labour supply and demand, and the implicit contract class of problem. The exclusion of the former is not so serious since a perfectly good survey of this area already exists (Hey, 1979a). The exclusion of the latter is regrettable and the time must come when stock should be taken of the results on incentive — compatability and risk-sharing contracts. In my view this interesting subject is still undergoing so many transformations as to make a survey premature. However, I hope the reader will agree that what remains of the theory of the labour market under uncertainty is both fascinating and insightful.

1 Search Processes

1.1 SEARCH PROCESSES AND DECISION RULES

Decision problems for economic agents are at the centre of the study of microeconomics. Agents endowed with known resources are confronted with a set of known market opportunities and must decide how to allocate the resources so as to maximise welfare (income, profit or utility). The models of microeconomics produce useful insights into the allocation and distribution of resources which result from agents' solutions to these problems. However, the anatomy of the decision itself as a time-consuming process is not needed, because the ingredient responsible for making decisions time-consuming and costly is missing. Uncertainty about the present and future (and the recent past!) market environment is what makes (for most of us) economic decisions troublesome. Buy a home computer now or wait for yet more price reductions and technological improvements? In a world of certainty of this type of decision is largely solved by appeal to the theory of inter-temporal consumption decisions and time preference. The problem changes dramatically for the consumer when the rate of technological advance or price decline is uncertain, and when the consumer is not even sure about what facilities or prices are currently available! Decision theory as a tool in economics really comes into its own in these circumstances. It forces us to pay closer attention to the decision itself, to specify correctly the agent's problem in terms of objective function, choice variables and the informational environment. On the last, we must establish how much is known about which variables and whether the agent can act so as to improve the state of knowledge.

Decision problems in which the agent is unable (or unwilling) to acquire additional information have been referred to as *passive* decisions (see Hey, 1981 for an outline and survey) while those in which agents may (at a cost) acquire more information have been termed *active* decisions. *Search processes* are the means by which information is discovered, and in this case a *decision rule* specifies the circumstances under which search for additional information will stop. This book is concerned with decision-making in active situations, and in particular those decisions made by agents which influence the workings of labour markets. Before we can make progress, however, I must make specific what is meant by search processes.

In fact, there are a very large number of ways in which search can take place, and associated with these are a large number of criteria which can be chosen to form decision rules — rules used to terminate the search for more information. In practice the potential sources of information are varied and large in number. Consider the home-computer problem referred to earlier. An active (search) decision problem here would be to discover more about current prices and technology. Leaving aside for the moment the problem of how much more information should be sought, we can first identify all the possible sources. In no particular order some of these would be:

reference to library copies of specialist magazines,
purchase of specialist magazines,
visits to stores,
direct application to manufacturers, and
information from friends, relatives and colleagues.

The different sources provide information of differing quality and reliability, and do so at different costs. The information gained from the last mentioned source, for example, costs almost nothing, but may be less reliable than that from the other, more expensive sources. Incidentally, that specialist magazines are available is a sign that there is a *market* for reliable information, and that some people are devoting resources to active search.

In labour markets too information and job opportunities

Table 1.1: Job-search methods

Job search method	Number using method	Percentage using method
Friend or relative	232	39.3
Advertisement	334	65.6
Notice at firm	61	10.3
Trade union	66	11.2
Employment service (state)	362	61.4
Casual application	217	36.8
Employment agency (private)	10	1.7

Source: Reid (1972), p. 483.

come from a variety of 'formal' and 'informal' sources. A 'formal' source would be a newspaper advertisement or job centre perhaps, while an 'informal' source would be word-of-mouth or through a 'grapevine'. In 'local' labour markets, information from the informal sources may be at least as reliable and probably much cheaper than that acquired from the formal sources. 'Job search' in its broad sense describes *any* information-gathering process leading workers to jobs, and typically workers use more than one search method. Table 1.1 is taken from Reid (1972) and reports a variety of methods used by a sample of male workers in locating jobs.

For the purposes of theoretical work however, more stylised concepts of job search are required. Furthermore, for the most part, I shall assume that only one method of job search is used by a worker. This keeps the central material of the book free from considerations about the choice of information sources, but does not mean that questions relating to an individual's choice over search methods are uninteresting. Any stylised concept of job search must specify (a) how search takes place, and (b) under what circumstances search will end. It will soon become clear that these two issues are related and can be settled only when the searcher's informational environment and constraints are identified. Clearly, a large number of possibilities exist.

1.2   OPTIMAL SEARCH PROCESSES

An *optimal* search process is one which, given a particular set of behavioural assumptions, maximises a specified objective function. Clearly, an optimal decision or policy is one which brings such a search process to an end in the 'best' way. The important point is that a policy is only optimal with respect to a particular set of behavioural assumptions. Under different assumptions, quite different policies may constitute *optimal* behaviour. To illustrate this point I shall study in some detail *two* ways in which information may be gathered, and *two* accompanying decision rules which maximise an objective function.

As a start, suppose that the searcher, new to the labour market, knows about what wages are available in the market but does not know where any particular wage offer is to be found. Each attempt to discover a wage offer involves a known fixed cost c, and the searcher prefers higher wages to lower wages. I ignore the problem of time and the individual's resources, and assume that each of the (large number of) firms in the market will make an offer if approached. How should the searcher gather the information? I consider two possibilities. First, that the searcher decides to select a particular number of firms and accepts the best wage to be found in the sample. Alternatively, the searcher decides on each 'visit' to a firm whether that offer should be accepted or rejected in favour of the opportunity to sample another firm. The first is called a *fixed sample size strategy* and the second, *a sequential search strategy*.

The common feature of both strategies is that search is random. There is nothing to distinguish firms *ex ante* and the searcher simply selects at random.[1] In addition, the reader can envisage *both* search strategies involving personal applications, telephone calls or visits to employment agencies. However, the two strategies are conceptually distinct because they imply different decision problems facing the searcher. In the first, the searcher must choose the sample size. In the second, some other criterion is used to bring search to an end, and by deciding which offers are 'acceptable', the number of searches is not predetermined.

Under each type of search strategy the worker has a decision problem — how much search should take place?

(i) The fixed sample size strategy[2]
The answer to the problem under the first mentioned

strategy is the choice of a sample size *prior* to search. For example, given knowledge of the distribution of wage offers and search costs, the worker can construct a table of expected returns and outlays associated with each possible sample size (see exercise 1.1). Suppose further that the searcher wants to maximise expected return *net* of search costs. The mechanics of the problem are as follows. Suppose that wage offers are distributed across all firms in the market according to the distribution fucntion $F(W)$ where W is the random variable wage offer and $F(W)$ has a density function $f(W) = F'(W)$. The wage offer is treated as a random variable (r.v.) because the searcher has no prior information on the location of any particular offer. I assume, though, that the searcher knows all there is to know about the form of $F(W)$ — for example, it could be a normal distribution or a Pareto distribution, and so on. How can the searcher use this information? It is clear that any random sample of wage offers will contain a maximum offer. It turns out that full knowledge of the distribution allows the searcher to calculate, for a given sample size n, the *expected* maximum wage offer in the sample, $E[\max W \mid n]$. Since the cost of collecting n wage quotes is cn, where c is the constant unit search cost, the *net* expected return from a sample of size n is at best:

$$R(n) = E\ [\max\ W \mid n] - cn \qquad\qquad (1.1)$$

Consider now the computation of the term $E\ [\max W \mid n]$. For a sample of size n, the probability that every observation is no greater than a number W is:

$$G_n(W) = Pr\ [w_1 \leqslant \mathrm{W}]\ Pr[w_2 \leqslant W]\ \dots$$
$$Pr[w_n \leqslant W],\ W \in [0, \bar{w}]$$
$$= F(W)^n$$

(which is the probability that W is the maximum of the sample). Also:

$$g_n(W) = G_n'(W) = nf(W)F(W)^{n-1}$$

and since any W is a potential maximum, the expected value of the maximum wage offer is:

$$E_n(W) = \int_0^{\bar{w}} Wg_n(W)dW$$

$$= n\int_0^{\bar{w}} Wf(W)F(W)^{n-1}dW,$$

which on integrating by parts (see the Appendix A.3) gives:

$$E_n(W) = \bar{w} - \int_0^{\bar{w}} F(W)^n dW \qquad (1.2)$$

Hence, $E[\max W \,|\, n] = E_n(W)$ given by (1.2). To see how $E_n(W)$ changes as the size of the sample increases note that:

$$E_{n+1}(W) - E_n(W) = \int_0^{\bar{w}} F(W)^n [1 - F(W)]dW$$

which is greater than zero for all n. This establishes that the expected maximum wage contained in a sample is greater the larger is the sample size. However, the increase in $E_n(W)$ falls with successive increases in n. In other words:

$$\Delta(n) \equiv E_n(W) - E_{n-1}(W)$$

is decreasing in n. Since $\Delta(n)$ is the incremental expected gain from increasing the sample from $n - 1$ to n it is worthwhile increasing the sample size as long as $\Delta(n) > c$. It is most certainly not worth increasing the sample to n if $\Delta(n) < c$. Thus, the optimal sample size n^*, is the *largest* integer satisfying:

$$\Delta(n) \geqq c. \qquad (1.3)$$

This model has several important features. First, having chosen n^* according to (1.3), the searcher must collect exactly n^* offers before making a choice. In particular the individual must not be deterred from carrying on the n^* if, say, the $(n^* - 2)$ offer is very large; nor must the search continue beyond n^* if all n^* offers have been meagre. Note that the inequality in (1.3) is just the 'marginal' condition associated with the maximisation of (1.1),[3] and we can establish from this (and the properties of $\Delta(n)$) that the optimal number of searches n^* increases (strictly, does not decrease) as c falls. Less search takes place if the cost of seach increases. This is a well-known and very important result.

(ii) The sequential search strategy

The fixed sample size rule is a little irritating. The idea that additional search costs should be incurred even if, before n^* offers have been collected, a 'very high' wage offer is found is frustrating and *seems* wasteful. Unfortunately, it is not obvious that changing the strategy mid-way is any less costly. The most likely alternative strategy used by a searcher is to decide after each solicitation whether the offer just received is in some sense 'acceptable'. Intuitively, the solution to this problem is made easier if the searcher can decide on a *minimally* acceptable wage offer. The sensible way to proceed would then be to reject all wage offers which fall short of this minimum wage or 'reservation wage', and to accept the first offer which is greater than or equal to the reservation wage. Naturally, this strategy only makes sense if the searcher can calculate the expected return for each conceivable reservation wage. The best or optimal reservation wage would then maximise the expected return net of search costs. Search continues only for as long as wage offers fall short of the reservation wage.[4]

To formulate the searcher's problem, assume the same informational environment as before; that is, the searcher knows everything about the distribution $F(W)$ of wage offers and the search cost. Again ignoring time and wealth considerations, I write the expected return to search when the reservation wage is r as:

$$R(r) = \int_r^{\bar{w}} Wf(W)dW + R(r)F(r) - c \qquad (1.4)$$

The first term on the right-hand side of (1.4) is the expected wage accepted multiplied by the probability that it is accepted (see the Appendix A.2 on conditional expectation). The second term is the return to search once more, multiplied by the probability that the wage solicited is not accepted — search takes place again if the current wage offer is rejected.

The final term, the search cost, is incurred whether or not the wage is accepted. Since the choice variable, the reservation wage, is continuous (rather than integer-valued) the derivation of the *optimal* policy is somewhat simpler than with the fixed sample size rule. Simply solve (1.4) for $R(r)$ and set $R'(r) = 0$. This implies that the optimal reservation wage, r^*, satisfies:

$$\int_{r*}^{\bar{w}} (W - r^*) f(W) dW = c \qquad (1.5)$$

which again is by way of 'marginal condition'. The right-hand side of (1.5) is the marginal cost of an extra search while the left-hand side is the marginal expected gain when the reservation wage is r^*. It can easily be verified that left-hand side of (1.5) is decreasing in r^*.[5] The implication is that if c increases, the equality in (1.5) can be maintained only if right-hand side also increases — *ceteris paribus* this requires a *reduction* in r^*. The reservation wage falls as the search cost rises. This is a very famous result. Furthermore because the probability of accepting a wage (and hence of terminating search) is $[1 - F(r^*)]$ a fall in the reservation wage increases the probability that search ends at any stage.

The sequential search model is the basis of the vast majority of the work on job search. Because of this I develop the model more carefully in the next chapter. The important point at the moment is not the *mechanics* of the solution but the general nature of sequential search.

Some detail of the mathematics of the fixed sample size rule and the sequential rule at this stage is necessary to emphasise the following important point. Because the informational environment permits expectations to be formed about the pay-off associated with either strategy, then either strategy can be used to maximise a well-specified objective function. However, are both strategies equally preferred?

It appears that intuitive misgivings about the fixed strategy are to an extent justified. Calculations by Feinberg and Johnson (1977) using specific functional forms for $F(.)$ — the normal and the rectangular distributions — show that, for the models developed in this section, the net expected return to sequential search exceeds that for non-sequential search.

In the notation of this section they show that:

$$R(n^*) < R(r^*) \qquad (1.6)$$

An important finding, though, is that the advantage of sequential search over the fixed sample rule varies as search costs vary. In particular $R(r^*) - R(n^*)$ is low for both 'high' and 'low' values of c and is higher when c takes moderate values. When c is very low, the implication of both strategies is that a large amount of search should take place, and when c is high the amount of search implied is very small. The recommendations of both strategies become very similar for high and low search costs. For moderate values of c the sequential rule's dominance is quite marked, and results from the fact that in this case the fixed sample size rule recommends 'too much' search, with respect to the expected gains contained in $F(W)$.

We conclude that *under current assumptions* the sequential rule dominates the fixed sample size rule. In fact the sequential rule is *optimal* under these assumptions. There are, however, circumstances under which the inequality in (1.6) may be reversed. For example, if there are economies of scale in search in which collection of a sample of observations can be made at substantially lower cost than the equivalent number of sequentially revealed observations, the fixed sample rule may be preferable to the sequential rule.

Other rules exist which may be preferred under different sets of assumptions. Gastwirth (1976) has brought attention to a decision rule which has features drawn from both the fixed sample rule and the sequential rule. The 'truncation rule' is to elect to search n times but if a wage in excess of a number d is found a truncation of the search is called for. If no wage greater than d is found search continues until n observations have been made, but does not continue thereafter. As intuition might suggest there is some saving in cost associated with this mixed strategy compared to the fixed sample rule. This rule too can be an *optimal* rule where expected net return is maximised by choosing the pair n and d.

Finally, the two search methods may be combined in the following way. Suppose time is divided into periods, but that *within* each period any number of wage offers may be solicited. In this case an optimal sample size may be chosen for within-period search while a minimum acceptable pay-off criterion may determine which period's search activity results in satisfactory return. Models of this type have been explored by Gal *et al.* (1981), Benhabib and Bull (1983) and Morgan (1983).

1.3 OPTIMAL *VS. AD HOC* PROCESSES

If optimal processes are so good, why use a non-optimal process? What are non-optimal processes? These questions can provoke a variety of responses only some of which I am directly interested in discussing here.

One response, for example, is that the 'real world' is too complicated to be modelled and that descriptive realism is lacking from the models described in the last section. This, of course, is a charge that can be levelled against all neoclassical models in microeconomics, and the answer to this criticism is well rehearsed. From the point of view of model-building the important issues are whether the theory captures the essential character of the problem (in this case uncertainty) and whether it succeeds in generating testable hypotheses.

Taking this argument as understood, it remains to establish both that the *essential* character of the problem has been captured and that the results can be tested against the available evidence.

To take the former and most involved issue first, it is clear that for *optimal* decisions to be made the net expected return calculation must be possible under the particular informational assumptions. The (common) informational assumptions underlying the models of the previous section did allow, both in principle and in practice, for the evaluation of the objective functions.

However, all is not well! Some would argue that as a representation of the essential nature of uncertainty, the assumption that searchers know *everything* about the distribution of wage offers is faulty. In practice and *in essence*, searchers in a market composed of a large number of firms cannot know all the details of the (objective) wage-offer distribution.

So, suppose that searchers behave *as if* $F(.)$ were the true, objective distribution, when in fact it is a subjective assessment of the true distribution, say $F^*(.)$, based on what little knowledge is available. This has an awkward corollary. If a searcher follows a strategy which is optimal with respect to $F(.)$ (and sticks to it), there is a risk (because $F^*(.)$ may be different from $F(.)$) that the strategy is in fact sub-optimal — that is, is not optimal with respect to the true distribution $F^*(.)$. Naturally, if learning about the true nature of $F^*(.)$ as search continues is impossible, or if search reveals (by chance) a frequency of offers perfectly consistent with the subjective evaluation $F(.)$, then the searcher can hardly be blamed for the sub-optimal behaviour. However, if the searcher, recognising that $F(.)$ and $F^*(.)$ may differ, makes inferences about $F^*(.)$ based on sample wage offers then *adaptive* behaviour is to be expected. Indeed a minimal requirement for 'rationality' would be that the searcher uses some rule to 'update' the subjective evaluation $F(.)$ in the light of seach experience. As $F(.)$ is adjusted so is the optimal strategy with respect to $F(.)$ — the searcher can do no better as long as 'best' use is being made of the available information. *Adaptive* behaviour then appears to be a natural accompaniment to subjective evaluation.

Unfortunately, the searcher's course is still far from clear. First, a rule must be chosen to update $F(.)$ in a systematic way making best use of the information contained in the wage offers. Bayes' theorem provides a way of doing this — at least in principle! Even so, for the Bayes' formula to be used the searcher must have an unshakeable and unchangeable view about the *general* form of $F^*(.)$; whether it is normal, for example, or belongs to a particular family of distributions. If this fundamental assumption about $F^*(.)$ is incorrect, the searcher is lost and Bayes is no help.[6]

Furthermore, in adaptive situations, although it may make sense to talk of an optimal strategy, it is unlikely that the strategy will take a form as simple as that involving, for example the reservation wage in the sequential search model.

When wage offers have a value as information as well as a value as potential income, it is not clear that a wage offer above a *particular* reservation wage is 'acceptable' if it is treated as a signal that the distribution is perhaps more favourable than previously thought. Search may continue in anticipation of even higher offers being found. The form of the 'optimal strategy' may be very complex. I return to this problem briefly in Chapter 3.

Finally, even if the searcher is *in principle* able to solve the problem optimally in an adaptive situation, the computational requirements may be immense. Again, the theorist could argue that the searcher behaves *as if* solving a complex adaptive search problem. The issue is really troublesome when the problem becomes so complex that even the theorist, with the aid of decision theory and computers, finds the calculation impossible or an extravagant use of time!

This line of argument has led repeatedly in the development of decision theory to investigations into the possible nature of 'reasonable' rules (rather than optimal rules) for terminating search processes. Although not totally arbitrary, these rules are in no way general. I therefore choose to call them *ad hoc*. In a world of 'sufficiently' informed searchers few economists would object to the optimal rules as an approximation of how search processes conclude. In a world of complete ignorance the tossing of a coin or some other random procedure would be good enough as a stopping rule. The middle ground is large. Experimental evidence shows that with very little information people make decisions not in a totally arbitrary way, but use various rules of thumb. There appears to be a fundamental desire by people to make good decisions if not optimal decisions. I list below two *ad hoc* rules which have been used by a group of individuals presented with a hypothetical sequential search problem.[7]

1. Have at least two searches, and stop if a wage is received which is lower than the previous one.
2. Continue searching as long as successive wages are higher by at least the cost of the search.

There are, of course, others. The second is particularly interesting since there is some attempt to take into account the cost of search. It is fair to conclude that if the same sequence of offers is received in two trials with different search costs, then the trial with the higher search cost will surely continue for no longer than the low-cost trial. This would be in line with the result from optimal search rules. In a variety of exercises set up by Schotter and Braunstein (1981) the responses of decision-makers approximates quite closely the predictions of optimal search models, including the result that higher search costs are associated with less search.

I now turn the opening question of this section on its head. If *ad hoc* rules are so reasonable, why worry ourselves with the technicalities of optimal rules — especially when the conditions under which the latter are truly optimal may not hold?

If the assumption of full knowledge about the wage-offer distribution is accepted as being an adequate representation of imperfect information, then the argument for the use of optimal rules is overwhelming. These rules dominate, in terms of expected costs, all *ad hoc* rules and are computationally fairly straightforward.

If the assumption of uncertainty surrounding the *form* of the wage-offer distribution is regarded as being more akin to an agent's actual environment, then since an apparently optimal rule runs the risk of being sub-optimal, a reasonable rule may be cost-saving. I take it, then, that if the assumption of subjectively-held beliefs about the wage offer distribution is adopted, then the possibility of agents using reasonable rules must be considered.

We have come far enough along this road. Experimenting with actual decisions continues to produce very interesting insights into economic behaviour, but it is not an appropriate starting point for a serious study of search theory.

The reader, hopefully, will soon realise that the biggest advances in this subject have used models of optimal behaviour. The techniques are powerful, and the results interesting. Furthermore, on available evidence[8] the results of the theory appear to be supported by laboratory experiments.

1.4 CONCLUSION

In the following chapter I enrich the sequential search model of section 1.2 just a little and derive the optimal policy more formally. Further elaborations of this model are considered in Chapter 3.

1.5 EXERCISES

1.1 Suppose a searcher faces the following distribution of wage offers and wants to maximise expected return by using a fixed sample size strategy as in section 1.2. How large is the optimal sample size when the search cost is (a) £3, and (b) £1?

Wage (£W)	Number of firms	Probability of obtaining each wage
120	2	2/144 = 0.0129
125	7	7/155 = 0.0452
130	14	14/155 = 0.0903
135	28	28/155 = 0.1806
140	40	40/155 = 0.2581
145	26	26/155 = 0.1677
150	20	20/155 = 0.1290
155	15	15/155 = 0.0968
160	3	3/155 = 0.0194
	155	

1.2 A searcher faces a rectangular distribution of wage offers given by:

$$f(W \mid a,b) = \begin{cases} 1/(b-a) & a \leqslant W \leqslant b \\ 0 & \text{otherwise} \end{cases}$$

and wants to maximise expected return using the sequential strategy of section 1.2. In this particular case the searcher knows that b = £60, and a = £20. What is the optimal reservation wage when the search cost is £2? What is r^* when c is £5?

2 Basic Model of Sequential Job Search

2.1 ASSUMPTIONS AND STRUCTURE

What I shall call the 'basic' model of sequential search contains the assumptions needed to generate a non-trivial search problem with no embellishments or institutional detail. More importantly, the choice of an alternative set of assumptions would complicate the model unnecessarily. Some alternative sets of assumptions are discussed in Chapter 3.

Given the very large number of possible assumptions that can be made (and have been made!), it is important to be clear about two things — the rules of the game and how the game is played. (In this case the 'gamester' is the job-searcher.) The rules are a list of assumptions fixing the job-searcher's environment, and this is accompanied by a 'story' outlining the *sequence* of events and the part played by the various assumptions. The assumptions of the basic model are the following:

(a) The job-searcher is unemployed, receives no unemployment benefit, has no budget or wealth constraint, and expects to live forever.
(b) A 'job' is characterised solely by a wage-rate offer.
(c) The searcher may select just one firm each period and inspect its wage offer at a constant known cost.
(d) Wage offers differ across (the large number of) firms and the firm inspected by the worker each period is selected at random. The distribution of wages across firms is known to the worker.
(e) The worker will take a job if and only if the wage offer belongs to a predetermined acceptance set. A wage offer

which does not fall into this set is rejected and the worker searches again in the following period.

(f)   The acceptance set is determined by maximising expected lifetime income. Search unemployment and employment at a chosen wage are the only alternatives open to the searcher.

(g)   Once a wage is accepted it is earned in each period in perpetuity.

I elaborate on these assumptions presently. Now for the 'story'.

The unemployed individual faces a continuous distribution of wage offers, and knows all the relevant facts about the distribution, including the minimum and maximum wage available, the average wage and other moments. Using this knowledge and knowledge of the cost of inspection, the individual calculates the expected net return to sampling from the distribution just once. What the searcher needs to establish is whether the wage offer which is solicited from the first randomly chosen firm is acceptable. Clearly, the individual could choose any arbitrary acceptance set and use this to calculate the expected net return to search. We assume though that an *optimal* acceptance set is used which *maximises* the expected net return. We study the details of the role played by the acceptance set in determining the expected return to search presently.

Having decided in *advance* which wages are to be acceptable (and hence which are not) the searcher selects a firm at random pays the cost of inspection and discovers the wage on offer at the firm. If the wage is found to be acceptable the worker takes the job and earns the wage rate forever from the beginning of the following period. Firms do not discriminate between applicants, do not vary the wage for the hired worker, and do not dismiss or even threaten dismissal. Workers earn the fixed wage in each period regardless of productivity (which is ignored completely in the basic model), and do not quit.

If the wage is found to be unacceptable the searcher, forfeiting the current period's search fee, searches once more in the *next* period, again paying a search fee. So the process continues. Search is terminated only by the acceptance of a wage offer by the searcher.

The assumptions enable us to keep the story simple (if a little hard to swallow as a description of a job market). Assumption (a) allows us to ignore the effect on the searcher's wealth on the cost and duration of search. If this were not the case, the searcher's choice of wage acceptance set would depend on the changing income and wealth position as (costly) search continues. We discuss the consequences of relaxing aspects of (a) in Chapter 3. Assumption (b) ensures that the searcher is concerned only about the wage on offer. There is no question of firms differing in terms of locality, quality - of the working environment or production technology. All workers are equally capable of filling vacancies. Assumptions (c) and (d) specify the search technology and the informational environment, from which it is clear (from the discussion of the last chapter) that the search process is sequential. Further, there is no uncertainty about the *distribution* of wage offers — the frequency of each wage offer is known — there is only uncertainty about *which* particular firms are offering which wages. Assumption (e) sets out the *stopping rule* for the search process. The search for a job stops when the observed wage is an element of the predetermined acceptance set; it is the determination of the acceptance set which is at the core of the search problem. Assumption (f) establishes the criterion used for determining the (optimal) acceptance set. The searcher maximises (makes the most of) the expected return to being in the current state — the state of search unemployment. Assumption (g) gives the return to a job once accepted.

Many of these assumptions may be changed whilst staying within the sequential search framework. Of course, then the story must be changed accordingly. I discuss some consequences of relaxing various assumptions in the next chapter.

I now make this outline of the basic problem more precise by putting together a mathematical formulation.

The searcher's problem is to maximise the expected return to search by choosing an acceptance set. Denote by $V(\mathcal{W}) > 0$[1], the expected return to search where $\mathcal{W}$ is the set of acceptable wages. Note that $V(\mathcal{W})$ is an *expected* return because at the moment the set is determined, the wage offer to be recieved is uncertain. I start by writing the expression for V ($\mathcal{W}$) and then explain the terms afterwards. We have:

$$V(\mathcal{W}) = -c + \frac{\varrho}{(1-\varrho)}\int_{\mathcal{W}} W dF(W) +$$

$$\varrho V(\mathcal{W})\left[1 - \int_{\mathcal{W}} dF(W)\right] \quad (2.1)$$

The first term on the right-hand side of (2.1) is the cost to the worker of inspecting a wage offer. Note that this is paid whether or not the offer is acceptable. The second term is the discounted expected earnings given that the wage offer is acceptable, multiplied by the probability that the wage is accepted (see the Appendix on conditional expectation). The final term is the discounted value of searching again in the next period, multiplied by the probability that the wage offer is not accepted. Hence, (2.1) may be written equivalently as:

$$V(\mathcal{W}) = -c + \frac{\varrho}{(1-\varrho)}E[W \mid W \in \mathcal{W}]Pr[W \in \mathcal{W}] +$$

$$\varrho V(\mathcal{W})Pr[W \in \mathcal{W}] \quad (2.2)$$

The expression for $V(\mathcal{W})$ — the return function — must allow for all possibilities. In this simple case, there are just two possible outcomes of this period's search: that the wage is accepted and earned in each period from the present onwards, and that the wage is not accepted so that search continues next period. The discounting procedure must reflect accurately the timing of the expenditures and receipts. The search cost this period c, is undiscounted since it is an immediate outlay. The expected earnings from accepting the solicited offer are earned in each period (excluding the current period) forever:

$$\varrho E[W \mid W \in \mathcal{W}] + \varrho^2 E[W \mid W \in \mathcal{W}]$$

$$+ \varrho^3 E[W \mid W \in \mathcal{W}] + \dots$$

$$= \sum_{t=1}^{\infty} \varrho^t E[W \mid W \in \mathcal{W}]$$

$$= \frac{\varrho E[\, W \mid W \in \mathcal{W}\,]}{(1 - \varrho)}$$

where ϱ is the discount factor (see the Appendix A.1 on discounting). If the current offer is rejected then search continues next period with expected return $V(\mathcal{W})$. However, as viewed from the *current* period, the present value of next period's return to search is $\varrho V(\mathcal{W})$. Equation (2.1) must first be solved for $V(\mathcal{W})$ to give:

$$V(\mathcal{W}) = \frac{\left\{ -c + \dfrac{\varrho}{(1 + \varrho)} \displaystyle\int_{\mathcal{W}} W dF(W) \right\}}{\left\{ 1 - \varrho \left[1 - \displaystyle\int_{\mathcal{W}} dF(W) \right] \right\}} \qquad (2.3)$$

The searchers problem is then to maximise (2.3) by choice of $\mathcal{W}$. We shall assume that the distribution function $F(W)$ of wage offers is continuous and defined for *all* non-negative wage offers. Since any w is an element of R^+ and an *acceptable* w is an element of $\mathcal{W}$, it follows that $\mathcal{W} \in R^+$; that is, the acceptance set is is a subset of the set of available wage offers. This is obvious — the searcher cannot find acceptable a wage which is unavailable. However, the precise form of $\mathcal{W}$ is less obvious. Exactly which wage will the searcher find acceptable? We establish this quite simply.

Suppose there is a wage offer $r \in R^+$ which, if received, makes the searcher indifferent between receiving r in perpetuity and continuing search next period, then r satisfies:

$$V(\mathcal{W}) = \frac{r}{(1 - \varrho)} \qquad (2.4)$$

Notice that $V(\mathcal{W})$ is constant. This is obvious from equation (2.1) and results primarily from the infinite horizon assumption which ensures that W is the same from one period to the next. Now it is clear from (2.4) that for *any* $w \geqq r$, the return to accepting w, $w/(1 - \varrho)$ is no less than $V(\mathcal{W})$, so that *accepting* $w \geqq r$ leaves the searcher *at least* as well-off as if search were continued. On the other hand for any $w < r$, the return from accepting w is lower than $V(\mathcal{W})$, so that the searcher is better-off searching and rejecting $w < r$. This important result suggests that the searcher adopts the following rule:

accept w if and only if $w \geqq r$ ⎫[2]
reject w if and only if $w < r$ ⎬   (2.5)

A search model for which (2.5) is the appropriate decision rule for the searcher is said to possess the *reservation wage property*, and r is known as the *reservation wage*. Some remarks about this famous result are in order.

First, the reservation wage property holds because the solution to (2.4), if it exists, is unique. This is because whilst the return to search is a constant, the return to accepting a wage offer w is greater the larger is w. Secondly, I have been at pains to *establish* the result in (2.5), not simply to assume it. There are many interesting search models which do not have the reservation wage property, either because the assumptions do not allow for the constancy of $V(W)$ (either with respect to the wage offer or over time), or because higher wage offers do not necessarily indicate better job offers. I give some examples in Chapter 3.

Finally, I have shown that *if* an r satisfying (2.4) exists then, given our assumptions, it is unique. Existence of such a wage is easily established and Figure 2.1 helps. Earlier, we

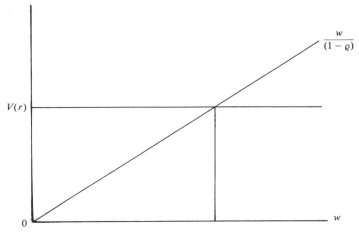

Figure 2.1: Existence and uniqueness of the reservation wage

specified the requirement that the expected discounted return from search, $V(\mathcal{W})$ be greater than zero. If $V(\mathcal{W})$ were less than or equal to zero then search would not be worth while and there would be no search problem! We also know that $V(\mathcal{W})$ is a constant under the current set of assumptions. On the other hand, the return to accepting a wage is strictly increasing in the wage offer with origin of zero. Hence given continuity of w and finite return to search $V(\mathcal{W})$ an r satisfying (2.4) exists. The argument is summarised in Figure 2.1.

2.2 THE SOLUTION

It is now clear from (2.5) that the acceptance set contains all of the wage offers above r and none below, so that the form of $\mathcal{W}$ has been established:

$$\mathcal{W} = \{W : W \geqq r\} \tag{2.6}$$

Which reads simply that the set of acceptable wage offers is composed of those wage offers no less than the reservation wage. This means that the conditional expectation and probability of acceptance can be re-written so that (2.3) becomes:

$$V(r) = \frac{-c + \dfrac{\varrho}{(1-\varrho)} \displaystyle\int_r^\infty W dF(W)}{[1 - \varrho F(r)]} \tag{2.7}$$

We now write $V(r) = V(\mathcal{W})$, since $\mathcal{W}$ is uniquely determined by the reservation wage. The searcher's problem is now to choose r so that (2.7) is maximised. It can easily be verified that the optimal value of r satisfies (as one might expect).

$$V(r^*) = \frac{r^*}{(1-\varrho)} \tag{2.8}$$

where $V(r^*)$ is (2.7) evaluated at $r = r^*$. The optimal reservation wage makes the searcher indifferent between accepting an offer equal to the reservation wage and continuing search. On combination (2.7) and (2.8) give:

$$c = \frac{\varrho}{(1-\varrho)} \int_{r^*}^\infty (W - r^*) dF(W) - r^* \tag{2.9}$$

which is essentially an equality between the marginal cost and expected marginal benefit of search.

2.3 PROPERTIES

Two very obvious properties can be determined quite easily. These concern the (comparative–static) effect of changes in the cost of search, c and in the discount factor ϱ. These results are obtained by substituting (2.8) into (2.7) (thus eliminating $V(\mathcal{W})$) and totally differentiating the resulting expression (2.9). This operation, which is routine gives:

$$\frac{dr^*}{dc} = \frac{\{-(1-\varrho)\}}{\{1 - \varrho F(r^*)\}} < 0 \tag{2.10}$$

$$\frac{dr^*}{d\varrho} = \frac{\left\{r^*F(r^*) + c + \int_{r^*}^{\infty} WdF(W)\right\}}{1 - \varrho F(r^*)} > 0 \tag{2.11}$$

An increase in the cost of search reduces the reservation wage. This result is very well known and has some interesting implications which we return to presently. The intuition behind the result is fairly clear. An increase in the cost of search makes continued search a relatively less attractive proposition than previously. The searcher would like to increase the probability of finding an acceptable wage offer. In this model this can be achieved only by enlarging the acceptance set and becoming less choosy. Consequently, the reservation wage falls.

The intuition behind (2.11) is equally clear. An increase in the discount factor is an increase in the weight attached to future rather than to present income. With a higher value of ϱ, the searcher is prepared to become more choosy by holding out for higher offers. Hence the reservation wage rises. This result is not particularly robust to changes in the discounting procedure. It is left as an exercise to establish what happens to (2.11) when the accepted offer is taken up *immediately* rather than at the beginning of the following period — all other assumptions remaining unchanged (exercise 2.1).

Further comparative–static exercises are possible if we allow the distribution of wage offers to change. There are clearly many possibilities here but some interesting results can be obtained even without assuming a particular functional form for $F(w)$. One interesting possibility is that $F(w)$ undergoes a transformation which affects the variance of offers but not the mean offer. Thus a *mean-preserving increase in riskiness* of the distribution increases the dispersion of wage offers with the mean unchanged. Let an increase in a parameter α have the effect of inducing a mean-preserving increase in risk. This is illustrated in Figure 2.2, where the effect on $f(w)$ and on $F(w)$ is shown:

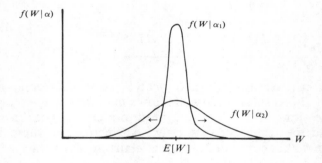

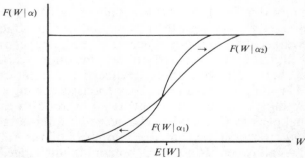

Figure 2.2: Mean-preserving increase in risk ($\alpha_2 > \alpha_1$)

Mathematically, we make use of the model of section 2.2 Rewrite (2.9) as:

$$c = \frac{\varrho}{(1-\varrho)} \left\{ \int_0^\infty W dF(W \mid \alpha) - \right.$$

$$\left. \int_0^{r^*} W dF(W \mid \alpha) - r^* [1 - F(r^* \mid \alpha)] \right\} - r^* \qquad (2.9')$$

By the definition of a mean-preserving effect, the first term in braces will not be affected by a change in α. Integrating the second term in braces by parts and simplifying, we have:

$$c = \frac{\varrho}{(1-\varrho)} \left\{ E[W] + \int_0^{r^*} F(W \mid \alpha) dW - r^* \right\} - r^* \qquad (2.9'')$$

from which it appears that:

$$\frac{dr^*}{d\alpha} = \frac{\dfrac{\varrho}{(1-\varrho)} \displaystyle\int_0^{r^*} \frac{\delta F(W \mid \alpha)}{\delta\alpha} dW}{\dfrac{\varrho}{(1-\varrho)} [1 - F(r^*)] + 1}$$

Under mean-preserving increase in risk the integral in the numerator of this expression is positive (actually non-negative) for all r^* (use Figure 2.2 to work out why), hence:

$$\frac{dr^*}{d\alpha} > 0$$

so that a mean-preserving increase in the riskiness in the wage-offer distribution increases the reservation wage.

At first sight this is a remarkable result — after all, our searcher here is a *risk-neutral* expected income-maximiser. Taken literally, this might seem to imply that the reservation wage is independent of α. That this is not so rests on the following intuition. A mean-preserving increase in the dispersion of $F(W)$ for a *given* reservation wage on the whole improves the distribution for wage offers above r^*. Although the mean of the distribution is unchanged, the conditional mean of *acceptable* wages has increased, improving the searcher's prospects and warranting an increase in the reservation wage.

The effect of changes in the reservation wage (resulting

from a parametric change) on the duration of search are also of interest. It is clear that since in each period the probability of finding an acceptable wage is $[1 - F(r^*)] \equiv p$, then $dp/dr^* < 0$. The probability that the search stops (by finding an acceptable offer) decreases with increases in the reservation wage. Similarly, the probability that search continues, $F(r^*)$, is positively related to changes in the reservation wage. It follows straightforwardly that the searcher can expect search to be more prolonged the higher is the reservation wage. Since wage offers are drawn at random from $F(W)$, the duration of search, identified in this model with the duration of unemployment, is uncertain. In fact the duration of search n is a random variable with a geometric distribution. The mathematical expectation of n is:

$$E[n] = \frac{1}{p} = \frac{1}{[1 - F(r^*)]} \qquad (2.12)$$

so that an increase in r^* increases the expected duration of search.

Returning to (2.10), as a consequence of an increase in the cost of search the fall in the reservation wage lowers the expected duration of search and hence (in this model) the expected duration of unemployment. This implication of the simple search model has been recognised for a long time and leads to the seductively simple policy conclusion that unemployment and the duration of unemployment among searchers can be reduced by increasing the search cost. Extending the model by allowing the worker to receive a per period constant unemployment benefit b, it can be established that r^* and $E[n]$ will fall if b is reduced. This is a routine exercise and is left to the reader. (Simply replace $-c$ in (2.7) by $-(c - b)$ and work through as before.) Notice the formal requirement that if the unemployment benefit is received whether or not the worker is engaged in search we require, for search to be worth while that $V(r) > b$. If, by not actively searching for a job, the worker would forgo the benefit payment we would require $V(r) > 0$ as before.

The policy conclusion, therefore, is that unemployment can be reduced by lowering the unemployment benefit payment. The result can also be obtained from neoclassical static microeconomics. A fall in *b* increases the opportunity cost of leisure and raises the relative attractiveness of work. The search explanation shows that, in so far as unemployment benefit acts as a search subsidy, the search process is likely to be shorter the lower is the unemployment benefit. Further, because the search theory does treat uncertainty in a systematic way, it allows for developments which include the incorporation of greater institutional detail. It is these developments which I consider in the remainder of the book. As you will see, it cannot be taken for granted that search behaviour always produces the results of this simple model.

2.4   PARTICIPATION

There is one further property of the model which I discuss separately here. The issue has been touched upon earlier, but is conceptually distinct from, and logically prior to, the decision to accept or reject job offers. It is the prior decision of whether to search at all! I have already hinted at the form taken by this decision. In short, the unemployed worker compares the expected return to search in the current period with the return to abstaining from active search. After all, in the presence of a search cost, the inducements offered by the wage distribution may not compensate and the individual may be better-off not incurring the search cost at all.

Notice that the participation decision — the decision to take an active part in the labour market, either as an unemployed searcher or as an unemployed worker — is not necessarily a once-for-all decision. In particular, if the non-participant's circumstances change, or if market conditions change, the individual may decide to switch from non-participation into active search. In other words, the participation decision for a non-participant receiving a social benefit payment of *b* is:

$$\text{participate in the current period if } V(r^*) > b \Big\}^3$$
$$\text{do not participate in the current period if } V(r^*) \leqslant b \Big\}$$

$$(2.13)$$

In our simple model there are no systematic inter-temporal variations in $V(r^*)$ or in b — both are constants so that, if it pays an individual to be a non-participant in the current period, it will always pay. Even so, the participation decision may be affected by changes in the search model's parameters. For the model which includes b in the way I suggested in the last section, any parametric change which increases $V(r^*)$ leaving b unchanged (for example, an increase in ϱ or decrease in c) makes participation more likely.

2.5   THE PRINCIPLE OF OPTIMALITY

In this section I consider an alternative method of solution to the simple search model. The method, which often proves useful particularly in more complicated models, uses the principle of optimality of dynamic programming.

The point of departure in terms of the earlier solution occurs with equation (2.1). The principle of optimality operates in the following way. Suppose that an optimal policy will be pursued should the worker be searching in the following period, then the current period's expected discounted return to search is:

$$V(r) = -c + \frac{\varrho}{(1-\varrho)} \int_r^\infty W dF(W) + \varrho V(r^*)F(r) \quad (2.14)$$

This reduces the problem to one of a single period, effectively assuming other periods out of the calculus by requiring optimality of all future decisions. If future decisions are optimal then the future return to search is $V(r)$ evaluated at r^*. As yet, of course, we do not know what the precise form of $V(r^*)$ is, nor do we know r^*. We do know that because of our assumptions the future values of $V(r^*)$ and r^* are the same as the current values. The procedure is now as before: maximising (2.14) with choice of r, and noting that $V(r^*)$ is a constant independent of r. The first-order condition implies that:

$$V(r^*) = \frac{r^*}{(1-\varrho)} \quad (2.15)$$

which is, of course, identical to (2.8). This is reassuring, and confirms that we have an alternative solution strategy which appears to be simpler than our earlier method, though the saving in computation time is more apparent in more complicated models.

2.6 CONCLUSION

This chapter has provided an important foundation for the remainder of the book. The main aim has been to develop the solution strategy for a simple search model and to insist that certain well-known properties of search models cannot be assumed to hold always, and so must be derived. The next chapter goes further and introduces important extensions to the basic model.

The results of the simple model have been rediscovered many times, though the discussion is often excessively technical. The basic source material for the results of this chapter are McCall (1970), Mortensen (1970) and Lippman and McCall (1976a). However, the first two models in particular have some differences in their treatment which are worthy of note. In McCall's model, the object of search is not a wage offer but a utility offer, where utility is a single-valued index summarising all benefits and disbenefits to a particular job. The problem is then to establish simply a reservation utility level. This is quite different from the problem, solved some years later, of deriving a *wage* acceptance set when the wage enters a (concave) utility function. I discuss this case in Chapter 3. In Mortensen (1970) an unemployed searcher samples randomly once in each period from a known stationary distribution of per period *relative* wages (the firm's wage offers relative to the market average wage), that is:

$$\int \omega dG(\omega) = \int dG(\omega) = 1$$

where ω is the random variable 'relative wage offer', and G its distribution function. The worker, as in this chapter, chooses r to maximise V over an infinite horizon. The most important feature of the Mortensen model, however, is that workers are not homogeneous, but are indexed according to a one-dimensional skill measure x. A job requiring a level of skill of at least x offers a wage $\omega(x)$, $\omega'(x) > 0$, (that is, once the worker observes the skill requirement the wage offer is known). For a worker of skill $\bar{x}$ the effective upper bound of wage offers is $\omega(\bar{x}) = \bar{\omega}$, hence the probability that a randomly selected offer is one for which the worker is qualified is:

$$\int_r^{\bar{\omega}} dG(\omega)$$

Most of the results of this chapter now follow. The reservation wage is equal to the present value of maximum expected future earnings and is constant over time. The reservation wage decreases with increased search costs and with a decreased discount factor.

Most of the early motivation for search models (as evidenced by the papers in Phelps *et al.*, 1970) was a theory of unemployment — and a theory of voluntary unemployment at that. It will be apparent after reading the next chapter that subsequent developments have made job-search theory a more general framework for the discussion of labour market dynamics.

Many of much-quoted results, such as the effect of reducing unemployment by reducing the search subsidy, often backfire on further examination (consider the implication of the result of exercise 2.2, for example) and must be treated tentatively. After all, the job-search model outlined here and its more elaborate extensions are essentially partial equilibrium models, and certainly do not tell the whole story.

This brings me to a vitally important issue, which I call 'the theoretical relevance of the job-search theory'. The problem concerns the distribution of wage offers in equilibrium. The assumptions set out at the beginning of the chapter, and in particular the implication of assumption (b) that all workers are identical and firms differ only in their wage offers, have an embarrassing implication when set in a market context, and when firms make well-behaved adjustments in their wage offers in response to the flow of labour generated.

If all workers are identical and face the same distribution

of wage offers they will surely all set the same reservation wage. As time goes on high-wage firms (i.e. firms offering wages above the common reservation wage) will find that they have no difficulty in filling vacancies and may well experiment with wage reductions. Meanwhile low-wage firms (i.e. firms offering wages below the common reservation wage) will find that they have no takers and must, if they are to produce at all, raise their wage offers. Eventually, with uninhibited wage adjustments and no random shocks to the system, firms will find that there is only one wage that need be offered to attract labour — the common reservation wage.[4] The consequence of this for the search model are devastating. With a degenerate distribution at the reservation wage the search problem disappears!

There are many ways round this problem, including continual exogenous random shocks, badly-behaved (or irregular) wage adjustment procedures by firms, and various types of heterogeneity.

Having pointed out the difficulty, I now ignore it and return to the problem in Chapter 4, since a full discussion is worth while only after firms' behaviour has been investigated.

Finally, there is the issue which I call[5] 'the empirical importance of the job-search theory'. A book on a theoretical topic such as job search would have limited appeal if it had no empirical relevance. The problem is one of measurement and of separating phenomena which are unmistakably features of search markets from those which have other, often simpler, explanations. I go into this more fully in Chapter 5. first, I shall tell my 'stories' and hope that they sound reasonable.

2.7 EXERCISES

2.1 Examine the impact of ϱ on r^* if the accepted wage offer is taken up immediately rather than during the following period. Explain the result.

2.2 Replace $-c$ in (2.7) by $-(c - b)$, where b is a state transfer to the unemployed whether actively searching or not, and let the participation decision be (2.13). How might manipulation of b affect the participation decision?

2.3   In the basic sequential search model the searcher is able to observe exactly one wage-offer in each period. Suppose, instead, that the searcher observes (receives) *at most* one offer. Let q be the exogenous probability that a wage-offer is observed. Provide an alternative formulation of (2.1) to allow for this new assumption for the case when (a) the search cost is paid regardless of whether an offer is received, and (b) the search cost is paid only if an offer is received. Establish that the model has the reservation wage property and investigate the impact of q on r^* for case (a) and for case (b).

2.4   Suppose that rather than facing an exogenous search cost c, searchers may choose search expenditure and by so doing can effect the probability of soliciting an offer q (introduced in exercise 2.3) according to the function $q = q(c)$ with $q'(c) > 0$. Examine the relationship between the optimally chosen value of c and r^* (continue to assume that there is no effective budget constraint), assuming that the search expenditure is incurred regardless of whether an offer is received.

2.5   Continuing with the model developed in exercise 2.4, make the adjustment suggested in exercise 2.2 by replacing the $-c$ term with $-(c - b)$. What effect does b have on (a) optimal search expenditure, and (b) on the probability of leaving unemployment?

2.6   Suppose that when the job is taken the worker is certain to earn in first period but in subsequent periods the job is terminated with (conditional) probability l. That is, l is the conditional probability that the job ends in any period given that it continued uninterrupted in the previous period. What is the effect of l or r^* if the worker does not return to search on termination of the job? (Think of l as the fatal job hazard probability.) You may assume that l is the same for all firms.

2.7   Consider the simple search model of section 2.2. Suppose that wage offers are distributed according to the Pareto distribution given by:

$$f(W \mid w_o, \alpha) = \frac{\alpha w_o^\alpha}{W} \text{ if } W > w_o$$

$$0 \quad \text{otherwise}$$

where w_o (>0) is the minimum wage available in the market (a constant) and $\alpha(>2)$ is a scale constant.

(a) Derive an expression for the reservation wage r^*.

(b) Determine the signs of dr^*/dc and dr^*/dw_o, and interpret the results.

(c) Derive an expression for the elasticity of r^* with respect to changes in c.

(d) Use the model to examine the effect of minimum wage legislation on the duration of unemployment.

3 Extensions

3.1 INTRODUCTION

I hope now that you have a grasp of the structure and solution of the simple job-search models. The exercises at the end of Chatper 2 should have helped by making relatively minor adjustments in the assumptions. The extensions I consider in this chapter are rather more significant. They do not change the fundamental structure of the job-search theory — all the models are recognisable as job-search models — but they do involve important adjustments to the way the problem is formulated. The richness of the job-search theory's results is enhanced substantially.

Each development is taken separately, partly because a 'grand synthesis' is a formidable task, but also to highlight the impact of each assumption on the model's results. It is perfectly natural that we should engage in the exercise of changing assumptions of the simple model. Not only does this model lack descriptive realism, but we know, even without subjecting it to test, that there are a large number of labour market features that it cannot capture. A moment's thought will reveal some of the very important features of labour markets which are missing. Leaving aside the matter of the firm's role which I turn to in Chapter 4, there are the issues of job changes, labour turnover, changes in the probability of leaving unemployment over a searcher's lifetime, and so on. The extensions of the basic job-search model discussed in this chapter shed some light on these issues. It is somewhat comforting that, as will soon become clear, it is possible to study a whole range of important labour market features from within the job-search framework.

3.2 CHOICE OF TIME HORIZON

In the basic model of Chapter 2 the time horizon is infinite. The searcher is assumed to live forever: the *possible* number of searches is infinite;[1] and a wage once accepted is received in perpetuity. Does this obvious lack of descriptive realism matter? Do the model's conclusions change if the infinite horizon assumption is replaced by an exogenous time constraint on search activity and employment duration? We have already seen in exercise 2.6 that *employment* duration may be exogenously determined by a random process *within* an infinite horizon model. For similar reasons an individual's demise may bring *search* to an abrupt, unplanned and unforeseen end! This is satisfactory as far as it goes, but it does not quite capture the idea of 'finiteness' of an individual's lifetime and the tendency for individuals, especially in later life, to recognise that earnings and consumption opportunities are diminishing.

An alternative way to proceed is to impose a known, fixed horizon on the individual's life. This is obviously an extreme assumption — the individual knows the predetermined life expectancy. However, the procedure does raise some quite general issues and produces interesting and plausible results.

As a start, note that one implication of the infinite horizon, constant cost and stable distribution assumptions underlying the model of Chapter 2 is that the expected return to search V, is constant in all periods. Relaxing any of these constancy assumptions raises the possibility that V changes in successive periods of search. This is most apparent if search cost c or the distribution $F(W)$ change over time because they directly affect the return to search V, and hence the optimal value of r, but it may also result from a finite search horizon. To see why, I develop a finite horizon model in this section.

The analysis is complicated considerably if we discount future earnings explicitly. These complications can be avoided initially by ignoring the discount rate entirely (in fact, let $\varrho = 1$). I shall return to this matter once the model of this section has been set out. Obviously the structure of this model is going to be somewhat different from the model of section 2.2

In the following ways the finite horizon model is going to be familiar. The individual searcher discovers exactly one wage offer at a constant known cost c. The solicited offer is drawn at random from the known, continuous distribution function $F(W)$. However, the individual's available time horizon is exactly T periods. This places both a limit on the possible number of searches and a limit on earnings potential once a job is accepted. An accepted job is taken until the worker retires at time T. Post-retirement income and wealth are zero.

The scheme, then, is as follows. A searcher enters the market at time $t = 0$ with the prospect of T periods of market activity. Since we allow (for simplicity) just one search each period, this puts a maximum of T on the potential number of searches. In addition, there is also a limit placed on a searcher's earnings potential — a wage w accepted in period $\tau(o < \tau < T)$ generates a total income of $w(T - \tau)$, while the same wage, if it were accepted a period later, would only generate a total income of $w(T - \tau - 1) < w(T - \tau)$. It is clear from this that the expected return to search at any point in time depends on the number of search opportunities remaining, and it is this fact which makes the finite horizon model so interesting.

To construct a finite time horizon model I shall use the general approach developed in Chapter 2; that is, in any period the searcher maximises the return to searching just once in that period, where *the return to search when* t *periods remain* is denoted by V_t. I shall also make use of the optimality principle and argue that, whatever acceptance criterion is used at time t, the decision at $t + 1$ will be optimal.

Strictly speaking, at this point I should establish what general form the acceptance criterion will take in any given period. However, a full discussion of this issue is useful only after the next section. For the moment, take it on trust that the model of this section is so structured as to make the following rule appropriate:

accept the wage offer w received when t periods $\Big\}$
remain if $w \geqslant r_t$
reject w otherwise and search again in the next
period

$$(3.1)$$

Of course, this is the reservation wage rule, where the subscript t allows for the possibility that the reservation wage r_t is appropriate only for the decision when t periods remain. It will be clear shortly both that the reservation wage rule is the correct rule and that the reservation wage used depends on how many periods of market activity remain.

An additional piece of notation will help. Let $U_t(w)$ be the total income when t periods remain if a wage w is accepted. In this model, where there is no discounting, $U_t(w) = tw$. I now write the return to search when t periods remain and a reservation of wage of r_t is used (as in 3.1)) as:

$$V_t(r_t) = -c + \int_{r_t}^{\infty} U_t(W)dF(W) + V_{t-1}^* F(r_t) \qquad (3.2)$$

The search cost is incurred unconditionally. If a wage is accepted, it is earned in each of the remaining t periods, taking account of the probability that $W \geqslant r_t$, this is the second term. Note from the definition of $U_t(w)$ that the second term in (3.2) is simply:

$$\int_{r_t}^{\infty} U_t(W)dF(W) = t\int_{r_t}^{\infty} WdF(W) \qquad (3.3)$$

If a wage is not accepted (with probability $F(r_t)$) then the searcher can earn at most V_{t-1}^* by searching (optimally) in the following period — when only $t-1$ periods remain.

It is apparent that the first-order condition for maximising (3.2) with respect to r_t implies that r_t^* satisfies:

$$U_t(r_t^*) = V_{t-1}^* \qquad (3.4)$$

and that on substituting (3.4) into (3.2) gives (after rearranging):

$$V_t^* = -c + \int_{r_t^*}^{\infty} [U_t(W) - U_t(r_t^*)] dF(W) + U_t(r_t^*) \qquad (3.5)$$

These general relationships will prove useful later. Equation (3.5) is the optimal return to search when t periods remain and, because of (3.4), this depends on (amongst other things) the expected return to search in the following period. V_t^* depends on V_{t-1}^* and also, since our choice of t is arbitrary, V_{t-1}^* depends on V_{t-2}^*, and so on. In the infinite horizon model this problem of *recursive* dependence did not arise since the model could be 'closed' by the fact that $V_t^* = V_{t-1}^* = V^*$, and hence could be solved for the single V^*. It would be wrong to close this finite horizon model in this way. There is no guarantee of a single unchanging V^*; in fact, there is a whole sequence of returns to search, $\{V_t^*\}_1^9$. On the face of it, there is little that can be said about (3.5) unless the model can be closed in some alternative way. Before I suggest a way of solving this unfamiliar system, notice that the condition (3.4) is actually very familiar. It states that the reservation wage should be chosen so as to make the searcher indifferent between accepting exactly r_t^* for the t remaining periods (with total income tr_t^*) and searching again in the following period. We appear to be on familiar territory after all!

One way to close a system such as that in (3.5) is to specify an 'end condition', and then the implications for the remainder of the sequence of V_t^*s can be traced back inductively. Consider the return to search when *no* periods of market activity remain. With no potential for earning anything it is clear that V_o is equal to the total post-retirement income. For simplicity let:

$$V_o = 0 \tag{3.6}$$

Hence write $V_1(r_1)$ as :

$$V_1(r_1) = -c + \int_{r_1}^{\infty} U_1(W)dF \tag{3.7}$$

this is the return to search when just one period remains, and clearly $U_1(w) = w$ by definition. The first-order condition for maximising (3.7) implies that $r_1^* = 0$ and hence:

$$V_1^* = -c + \int_o^{\infty} WdF(W) \tag{3.8}$$

This result is clearly sensible. The best the worker can do if only one period remains is accept *any* wage offer as long as $V_1^* > 0$. I shall *assume* that (3.8) is positive. Now from (3.4):

$$U_2(r_2^*) = V_1^* \qquad (3.9)$$

that is:

$$2r_2^* > 0$$

and so by assumption that $V_1^* > 0$:

$$r_2^* > r_1^* = 0 \qquad (3.10)$$

This is an immediate and important implication of the condition that $V_o = 0$ and $V_1^* > 0$. The critical issue is what these conditions imply for the entire sequence of V_t^*s and r_t^*s. The inductive argument proceeds in three stages. First, I find a general condition on the V_t^*s which will make (3.10) true for any t and $t - 1$, that is, $r_t^* > r_{t-1}^*$. Secondly, I establish whether $r_t^* > r_{t-1}^*$ implies that $r_{t+1}^* > r_t^*$ for any t. Finally, I establish whether the condition discovered in the first stage is true for one t.

1. From (3.4):

$$V_t^* - V_{t-1}^* = U_{t+1}(r_{t+1}^*) - U_t(r_t^*)$$
$$= (t + 1)r_{t+1}^* - tr_t^* \qquad (3.11)$$

Now let:

$$V_t^* - V_{t-1}^* > r_t^* \qquad (3.13)$$

hence:

$$(t + 1)r_{t+1}^* - tr_t^* > r_t^* \qquad (3.14)$$

and so:

$$r_{t+1}^* > r_t^* \qquad (3.15)$$

In general, then, the reservation wage will fall between period $t + 1$ and period t for sure if $V_t^* - V_{t-1}^* > r_t^*$. Condition (3.13) is sufficient for (3.15).

2. I need to show that if

$$V_t^* - V_{t-1}^* > r_t^* \; (r_{t+1}^* > r_t^*)$$

then:

$V_{t+1}^* - V_t^* > r_{t+1}^*$ (and hence that $r_{t+2}^* > r_{t+1}^*$) for *any t*.

To ease notation define:

$$\Delta_t \equiv V_t^* - V_{t-1}^* \tag{3.16}$$

Now, using (3.5):

$$\Delta_{t+1} = (t + 1) \int_{r_{t+1}^*}^{\infty} (W - r_{t+1}^*) dF(W) -$$

$$t \int_{r_t^*}^{\infty} (W - r_t^*) dF(W) + \Delta_t \tag{3.17}$$

and using (3.12) and rearranging gives:

$$\Delta_{t+1} = t \left\{ \int_{r_{t+1}^*}^{\infty} (W - r_{t+1}^*) dF(W) - \int_{r_t^*}^{\infty} (W - r_t^*) dF(W) \right\}$$

$$+ t(r_{t+1}^* - r_t^*) + \int_{r_{t+1}^*}^{\infty} (W - r_{t+1}^*) dF(W) + r_{t+1}^* \tag{3.18}$$

By assumption, $r_{t+1}^* > r_t^*$, and so the second line of (3.18) is certainly positive. However the first term on the first line is negative. Now if $r_{t+1}^* = r_t^*$ the first term on the first line is zero, and as r_{t+1}^* increases (r_t^* unchanged) by dr_{t+1}^* this term *falls* by $t[1 - F(r_{t+1}^*)] dr_{t+1}^*$. But the second term on the first line which is also zero for $r_{t+1}^* = r_t^*$ increases (as r_{t+1}^* increases) by $tdr_{t+1}^* > t[1 - F(r_{t+1}^*)] dr_{t+1}^*$. So the second term on the first line which is positive if $r_{t+1}^* > r_t^*$ is always larger than the first (negative) term for any $r_{t+1}^* > r_t^*$. Hence:

$$\Delta_{t+1} + r_{t+1}^* > 0$$

and the result is established. *If $r_{t+1}^* > r_t^*$ then $r_{t+2}^* > r_{t+1}^*$,* for any *t*.

To summarise so far, I have shown that for any *t*:

1. *if $V_t^* - V_{t-1}^* > r_t^*$, then $r_{t+1}^* > r_t^*$,* and

2. if $r_{t+1}^* > r_t^*$, then $r_{t+2}^* > r_{t+1}^*$.

I now only need to show that $V_t^* - V_{t-1}^* > r_t^*$ is indeed true for one *t*.

3. I shall show this for $t = 2$; that is, I want to show that $\Delta_2 > r_2^*$.

$$\Delta_2 = \int_{r_2^*}^{\infty} [U_2(W) - U_2(r_2^*)]\,dF(W) + U_2(r_2^*) - \int_o^{\infty} W\,dF(W)$$

$$= 2\int_{r_2^*}^{\infty} W\,dF(W) - 2r_2^*[1 - F(r_2^*)]$$

$$+ r_2^* - \int_o^{r_2^*} W\,dF(W) - \int_{r_2^*}^{\infty} W\,dF(W)$$

$$= \int_{r_2^*}^{\infty} (W - r_2^*)\,dF(W) + \int_o^{r_2^*} (r_2^* - W)\,dF(W) + r_2^*$$

hence:

$\Delta_2 - r_2^* > 0$, and so $r_3^* > r_2^*$.

The solution is now complete. We have established that $r_2^* > r_1^*$ (trivially), $r_3^* > r_2^*$, and that if $r_t^* > r_{t-1}^*$ then $r_{2+1}^* > r_t^*$ for any t. It therefore follows that *for all* t:

$$r_t^* > r_{t-1}^* \tag{3.19}$$

The method of arriving at (3.19) may appear to be tortuous, but it is actually quite straightforward. (Figure 3.1 will help.) You will see that given the series of $U_t(W)$ functions, $V_t^* > V_{t-1}^*$ is not sufficient to guarantee that $r_{t+1}^* > r_t^*$. In fact the V_t^*'s must be further and further apart the higher is t. In essence this is exactly what has been demonstrated.

The result in (3.19) is justly the most famous of finite horizon models. It clearly makes intuitive sense. The searcher *systematically* becomes less choosy about acceptable wages as time runs out. In terms of the probability of accepting a wage p_t, it is clear that:

$$p_t = [1 - F(r_t^*)] < p_{t-1} = [1 - F(r_{t-1}^*)]$$

so that the probability of accepting a job when t periods remain is lower than when only $t - 1$ periods remain. Of course, when only one period remains the individual will accept any job:

$$p_1 = [1 - F(o)]$$
$$= 1$$

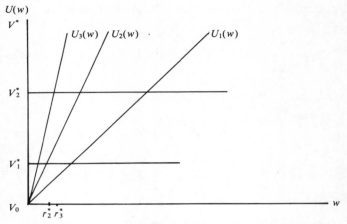

Figure 3.1: The falling reservation wage

The implications of this, of course, is that *ceteris paribus* an individual who is a relative newcomer to search experience is less likely to accept a job than is an identical person who has been searching longer.

Adventurous readers may choose to verify the following results for themselves. An increase in the per period cost of search c, lowers r_t^* for all t.[2]

The results of this section have been derived using the method of solution developed in Chapter 2. However, many expositions of the finite horizon model have adopted a subtlely different approach (see Lippman and McCall, 1976a) and for completeness I shall outline this now. The key to this alternative approach is to calculate, not the expected return to search before search takes place, but the expected return when a particular offer has just been received and is being held by the searcher.

Denote by $\tilde{V}_t(w)$ the *maximum* expected return when t periods remain and an offer w is currently held, then:

$$\tilde{V}_t(w) = \max\left\{tw, -c + \int_0^\infty \tilde{V}_{t-1}^*(W)dF(W)\right\} \qquad (3.20)$$

and let the terminal condition be:

$$\tilde{V}_1^*(w) = \max\{w, 0\} \qquad (3.21)$$
$$= w$$

(There is no return next period and the search cost is not incurred.)

It is clear from (3.21) that any wage is accepted when just one period remains and so $r_1^* = 0$; that is, r_1^* is the value of w which equates the two terms in braces on the right-hand side of (3.21). It is also clear from (3.20) that the expected value of $\bar{V}_{t-1}^*$ is unaffected by the current value of w on offer and that the higher is the currently available w the better-of is the searcher. Hence the reservation wage rule is appropriate. As with (3.21) the reservation wage in t equates the two terms in braces on the right-hand side of (3.20). The reservation wage make the searcher indifferent between acceptance and rejection, and so r_t^* satisfies:

$$tr_t^* = -c + \int_0^\infty \bar{V}_{t-1}^*(W)dF(W) \tag{3.22}$$

The results of this section now follow from (3.20)–(3.22) by induction.[3] The results also hold for $o < \varrho < 1$, but the proof is somewhat more involved.

The participation decision must also be reviewed in the context of the finite horizon model. In the simple model of Chapter 2 the participation decision had a natural interpretation but was rather uninteresting in view of the constancy of the returns to market activity relative to non-market activity. In other words, a worker for whom the returns to search were greater than the return to non-market activity would *always* participate. The participation decision is much more interesting in the finite horizon model and has been studied by Pissarides (1976b) in a model which is somewhat richer in detail than the finite horizon model of this section. A permanent move into non-participation is determined by the worker's choice of a search horizon which is less than the individual's (finite) lifetime horizon, a distinction not made in the model of this section. Temporary transitions into and out of participation are produced by inter-temporal variations in the search model parameters (search cost, wage-offer distribution and discount rate). Of particular interest is the effect of an improvement in wage offers expected sometime in the future. Even if the current wage-offer distribution is unchanged, the prospect of higher future income will raise *current* reservation wages. Searchers may save on search costs by abandoning active search temporarily and rejoining the market when the wage improvements are imminent. Hence the concepts of the 'added worker' and 'discouraged worker' familiar to labour economists have a quite natural job search interpretation.

3.3   THE RECALL PROBLEM

The fact that the reservation wage falls in the model of the last section implies that as time passes wage offers previously considered to be unacceptable become acceptable — until eventually (if search has not stopped) *all* offers are acceptable. However, an important issue has been deliberately side-stepped concerning the availability of previously rejected offers. In the last section I implicitly assumed that an offer, once inspected and rejected in favour of continued search, was lost or unavailable. Future offers could only be generated by searching afresh and sampling from $F(W)$, and could not be 'stored up'. In other words, in the model of the last section there is *no recall* of previously discovered wage offers.

Where recall is allowed, the problem of stopping the search and selecting the best offer is much more complicated. In fact, at any point in time there are *potentially* three possibilities for the searcher: continue search, accept the current offer, or recall a previous offer. Assuming that *all* previous offers are available at no extra cost, the only offer worth recalling is the *maximum* of all previous offers.

Let z_t be the maximum of the sequence of offers from the time when T periods remain to time t, *viz.*:

$$z_t \equiv \max\{w_T, w_{T-1} \ldots, w_t\} \qquad (3.23)$$

Now, suppose at time t there is a reservation wage $\tilde{r}_t^*$ which makes the following rule optimal:

accept the current offer w_t if $w_t > \tilde{r}_t^*$
reject the current offer w_t if $w_t \leqslant \tilde{r}_t^*$

According to this, *any* offer greater than $\tilde{r}_t^*$ should be accepted. However, if a particular wage offer w_t both exceeds the value $\tilde{r}_t^*$ and is also the largest offer so far received, it can be stored, increasing the expected return to continued search since in the future it will be there to fall back upon. Hence, a particularly high wage offer may be rejected and stored because it raises the return to *search*. In this case $\tilde{r}_t^*$ is not after all a reservation wage, and since the generation of wages is random, it is not clear that *any* pre-assigned reservation wage rate makes any sense when recall is allowed.

In their survey, Lippman and McCall (1976a) demonstrate that if search takes place over total discounted income offers y, and these are independently and *identically* distributed in each period according to a distribution function $G(.)$, then with recall a reservation value of y exists in each period and is *constant* over time at a value that would result from an infinite horizon model.[4] Their equivalent of (3.20) in this case is:

$$\bar{V}_t^*(y) = \max\{y, \quad -c + \bar{V}_{t-1}^*(y)G(y) + \int_y^\infty \bar{V}_{t-1}^*(x)dG(x)\}$$

(3.24)

The second term, which is the return to search when $t-1$ periods remain, takes account of the fact that since y can be stored, the searcher who finds an offer less than y (which probability $G(y)$) next period can do no worse than receive $\bar{V}_{t-1}^*(y)$. The final term is the expected return given that an offer in excess of y is found multiplied by the probability of this occurring.

The result of the constancy of the reservation total income arises because there is no deterioration in the total income of previously discovered offers. A total income of £y discovered two periods ago (for example) and stored up is still worth £y. Furthermore, the income offer distribution does not deteriorate over time. The effect is for earnings opportunities not to diminish with the passage of time. this is clearly an unsatisfactory feature for a finite horizon model, and for this reason we should not set too much store on this result.

The recall problem has been studied further in the hope of producing a more general formulation in which no recall and perfect (full) recall may be seen as extremes. In practice rejected employment opportunities *may* be available in the future but are not *certain* to be so. To model partial recall would be desirable to make the theory more general — the two extremes being special cases. Two attempts, neither of which are totally satisfactory, have been made to formulate this problem.

In a model not directly related to the simple models under study here, Karni and Schwartz (1977) specify partial recall to mean that an offer observed τ periods ago is available now with probability $p(\tau)$ known to the searcher. Using a special case it is found that the reservation wage[5] under partial recall is bounded above by the reservation wage under perfect recall and is bounded below by that under no recall.

At about the same time, Landsberger and Peled (1977) settled on the following specification (adapted here from their consumer-search framework to the job-search framework). As search proceeds and the sequence z_t (in (3.23)) is generated, then at a point $t - 1$ periods away from the horizon z_t is available with probability p. No other past offer is available except the maximum of all previous offers, and that always with a probability p. This is an uncomfortable assumption since, if anything, we would expect higher offers to be more likely to disappear from the market. That z_t is available with the same probability now as it will be next period is unlikely to be a feature of a market composed of a significant number of searching workers.

These attempts, despite their shortcomings, have yet to be improved upon. Most desirable would be a formulation in which the probability that a previous offer is available depends both on its magnitude and the time elapsed since inspection. This would introduce interesting trade-offs for the searcher, but the mechanics of the problem appear to be daunting.

3.4   ON-THE-JOB SEARCH

So far I have considered the structure of the job-search problem from the point of view of an unemployed worker. The possibility that a worker may search for a (better) job while employed takes us nearer to the circumstances faced by many workers,[6] and poses new and interesting problems for the theorist.

Initially, I shall ignore the problem that job changes themselves may be costly, and simply continue to assume that it is the search cost which constrains the searcher.

(i) Costless job-changes

At any point in time a worker has three options regarding search and work, these are: (1) search and do not work, (2) work but do not search, and (3) work and search. The first two only have been assumed possible hitherto. The introduction of the third possibility considerably complicates the strategies employed by agents. I shall outline but not detail a model due to Burdett (1977, 1978) (see also Hey, 1977).

The new strategies are derived for an employed searcher, and the model is one of a finite horizon with recall. Let U_{it}, $(i = 1, 2, 3)$ be the expected maximum return to choosing option i in any period. Let w be the current wage received in each period, or the highest offer received so far depending on whether the worker is employed or unemployed. The search cost incurred when unemployed and employed are c_1 and c_2, respectively. The expected maximum discounted net income for a worker currently with the opporutnity of earning w when t periods remain is:

$$V_t^*(w) = \max\{U_{1t}(w, c_1), U_{2t}(w), U_{3t}(w, c_2)\} \qquad (3.25)$$

and, ignoring unemployment benefit we have:

$$U_{1t}(w, c_1) = -c_1 + \varrho \int_w^\infty V_{t-1}^*(W)dF(W)$$
$$+ \varrho V_{t-1}^*(w)F(w) \qquad (3.26)$$
$$U_{2t}(w) = w + \varrho V_{t-1}^*(w) \qquad (3.27)$$
$$U_{3t}(w, c_2) = w - c_2 + \varrho \int_w^\infty V_{t-1}^*(W)dF(W)$$
$$+ \varrho V_{t-1}^*(W)F(w) \qquad (3.28)$$

In (3.26) the unemployed searcher currently holding a best offer of w available with perfect recall pays a search cost c_1 and expects to receive next period a higher wage offer generating an expected income given by the second term, or to be no worse-off than at present if no improved wage offer is found given by the final term.

In (3.27) the employed worker earning w per period is not searching so that the interpretation of the left-hand side is obvious.

In (3.28) the worker employed at w also searches, paying a cost c_2 and may find a wage improvement (the second term) or be no worse off if a lower wage than the one currently earned is found.

As we shall see, this system generates *three* different reservation wages.

Finally,

$$V_1^*(w) = U_{21}(w) = w \tag{3.29}$$

and

$$V_o^* = 0$$

Then, using (3.26)–(3.29) we find that for any w and $t > o$, $\partial U_{2t}/\partial w > \partial U_{3t}/\partial w > \partial U_{1t}/\partial w > o$. Now, let z be the value of w which makes the worker indifferent between options (1) and (3), x_t be the value of w which makes the worker indifferent between options (1) and (2), and y_t be the value of w which equates U_{2t} and U_{3t}. Then $z \gtrless z_t$ if and only if $y_t \gtrless x_t$, from which it follows that, if $z \leqslant x_t$ the following strategy is adopted:

$$\left. \begin{array}{l} \text{Search and do not work if} \quad w < z \\ \text{Work and do not search if} \quad w \geqslant y_t \\ \text{Work and search if} \qquad z \leqslant w < y_t \end{array} \right\} \tag{3.30}$$

If, on the other hand, $z > x_t$, the following strategy is appropriate:

$$\left. \begin{array}{l} \text{Search and do not work if} \quad w < x_t \\ \text{Work and do not search if} \quad w \geqslant x_t \end{array} \right\} \tag{3.31}$$

In other words, simultaneous work and search is ruled out (as in the simple models) only if $z > x_t$.

The argument is very clearly stated in Burdett (1978), who goes on to derive the implications of this scheme for quit behaviour. This is an important use of the model. This is our first example of a search model which is capable of generating quits; for workers who are searching and working there is a non-zero probability that they will find and *accept* an improved wage offer in any period.

(ii) Costly job-changes

Of course, the conditions of acceptance of an improved offer change if the cost of acceptance is at all significant. After all, taking up a new job often involves disruption and possibly a costly move. Hey and McKenna (1979) have reversed these cost assumptions by making *search* costs zero and moving costs c_m positive. For a worker currently earning w per period and receiving one offer each period[7] the following decision strategy is used. For an offer w_o and a current wage w, there is a function $v(w)$ such that the worker should;

$$
\begin{rcases}
\text{move (that is, accept } w_o) \text{ if } w_o \geqq v(w) \\
\text{not move (reject } w_o) \text{ if } \quad w_o < v(w)
\end{rcases}
\tag{3.32}
$$

Naturally, the exercise involves establishing the properties of the critical value function $v(w)$. First, optimal behaviour is found by maximising total discounted expected income net of moving costs. Specifically, the problem is;

$$
\max_{v(w)} V(w) = w + \varrho \left[V(w)F(v(w)) \right]
$$

$$
+ \varrho \int_{v(w)}^{\infty} [V(x) - c_m] \, dF(x)
\tag{3.33}
$$

The solution, $v^*(w)$ satisfies:

$$
V^*(v^*(w)) - c_m = V^*(w)
\tag{3.34}
$$

so that the worker is indifferent between continuing to earn w and accepting (i.e. moving for $v^*(w)$). Details of the analysis are to be found in Hey and McKenna (1979), but one result easily stated here is that the critical wage function $v^*(w)$ shifts upwards as the moving cost increases, or:

$$
\frac{\partial v^*(w)}{\partial c} > o \text{ for all } w.
\tag{3.35}
$$

Hence, the worker is more reluctant to move the higher is the moving cost, a result with a clear intuitive appeal.

Of greater interest is the result that low-wage individuals require a *larger* financial inducement to move than do high-wage individuals, even though they may have the same search cost. This somewhat startling implication arises from the fact that since low-wage workers (in this model) have the greatest scope for wage improvement they are relatively reluctant to move. This is to guard against the possibility that an even higher wage may be discovered after the move which would have been acceptable prior to the last move, but is not sufficient now to justify yet another move. Low-wage workers are more likely to suffer from this than high-wage workers — hence the result. Mathematically, this means that $(V^*(w) - w) > 0$ is decreasing in w.

3.5   EXPECTED UTILITY MAXIMISATION

With little justification, I have been concerned with the job-search problem seen through the eyes of an expected (discounted) income maximiser. The principal justification for this is simplicity. In a trivial way, we could always redefine the wage offer to be a utility offer. As long as the per period utility offered by a job could be discerned simply by inspection search theories outlined so far may simply be reinterpreted to be concerned with search for utilities not simply for wages (Kohn and Shavell, 1974).

Somewhat less trivially we may persist in searching for wage offers but translate a wage offer received into a welfare level, according to a known function $U(w)$. The wage is therefore no longer a direct measure of individual welfare. Results then hang on the form of $U(w)$. Hall *et al.* (1979) have considered this case.

In an infinite horizon model a searcher searches for total income offers (as in the Lippman and McCall (1976a) paper referred to earlier). However, allow utility to depend also on wealth net of search costs and define; $V^*(M)$ to be the maximal expected utility from continued search when wealth is M, and $U^*(M + y)$ the expected utility from an income y

when wealth is M. Now:

$$V(M) = \int_0^\infty \max\{U^*(M - c + x), V^*(M - c)\}dG(x)$$

$$(3.36)$$

and the appropriate acceptance criterion is:

$$\begin{array}{l} \text{accept } y \text{ if } U^*(M - c + y) \geqq V^*(M - c) \\ \text{reject } y \text{ if } U^*(M - c + y) < V^*(M - c) \end{array} \quad (3.37)$$

Two questions naturally arise in this model. First does the decision in (3.37) involve the use of a unique reservation value of y for each level of wealth, say $y^*(M)$? Secondly, what is the effect on search behaviour of an increase in wealth? The answer to the first of these is yes. In the case of expected utility maximisation without recall and with an infinite horizon the reservation wage (income) property holds. The answer to the second question depends on what assumptions are made about the effects of changes in wealth on utility. In short, if $U(.)$ exhibits decreasing absolute risk-aversion[8] then the reservation wage increases with wealth, and hence the searcher becomes more selective (Hall *et al.*, 1979, theorem 10, p. 154).

As we expect, with recall the utility-maximising case becomes more involved. In general, the existence of a reservation value $y^*(M)$ cannot be guaranteed.

However, it is apparent that the expected income-maximising framework is a special case of expected utility-maximisation — the case of a utility function linear in income (and wealth). This leads to the following result. Consider only utility functions exhibiting decreasing absolute risk-aversion. If $Y(M)$ is the set of all acceptable offers under expected utility-maximisation when wealth is M, and recall is allowed (not allowed), then $Y(M)$ contains the set of offers acceptable under expected income-maximisation when recall is allowed (not allowed). For the case of no recall this implies that:

$$y^* \geqq y^*(M) \qquad (3.38)$$

A risk-averter with wealth M is less selective than an expected income (risk-neutral utility)-maximiser.

Finally, in the case of recall, the set of acceptable incomes *increases* as search continues under expected utility-maximisation (with risk-aversion) in contrast to the expected income-maximising case summarised in equation (3.24).

The question of what happens to a searcher's reservation wage when the distribution of offers undergoes an increase in risk was first raised in Chapter 2. McCafferty (1979) has studied this problem for the case of expected utility-maximisation. Using a specific form for the distribution of wage offers, it appears that an increase in the variance of the (uniform) distribution with the mean unchanged will lead to an increase in the reservation wage even for some risk-averse individuals. We saw in Chapter 2 that risk-neutral expected income-maximisers respond in this way. It seems that searchers must have quite a high degree of risk-aversion before an increase in wage dispersion causes them to lower reservation wages.

3.6   RESIDUAL UNCERTAINTY

The theory so far developed has relied exclusively on the idea that the search process itself reveals all job characteristics of interest to the searcher. As long as we confine ourselves to search for wage or income offers this assumption of discovery by *inspection* is reasonable. However, by broadening the interpretation of a job offer to include non-wage characteristics (that is, to search over job utility offers) it is appropriate to question whether all job attributes which may affect total utility are observable by inspection. This problem was first noted by Borjas and Goldberg (1978). The consequences of assuming that search cannot reveal all of the job's features and that there is some *residual uncertainty* are important. A search model can be developed which takes account of the fact that some job attributes may be discovered only if they are *experienced*; and they can only be experienced if a job is accepted — at least on a temporary basis.

It is convenient to think of a job as offering a total utility package, but where 'utility' is composed of a wage offer w, and a money equivalent of the utility value of the other job characteristic s. Here the assumption is that the wage is the inspection characteristic (as in the simple job-search model), while s is the experience characteristic. The total job package is worth $u = w + s$; however search can take place only for wage offers (since only these are observable) and so we can anticipate that the solution to this problem will depend on the information about s (and hence u) contained in the observed wage offer.

Another consequence of this new assumption may also be anticipated. If the initial job acceptance decision depends on w, as it must, then higher wage offers will only be preferred to lower offers if they are not associated with lower expected job utility values. I shall make this more specific presently, but it is apparent that the reservation wage rule need not be appropriate. For this reason I shall set up the problem in terms of a general wage acceptance set, $\mathcal{W}$. To keep the analysis simple, I assume an infinite horizon, a constant search cost c and a discount factor ϱ. In the spirit of the literature which has developed on this problem, I shall allow the worker to quit after one period in a job, this being the assumed length of time it takes for a worker to evaluate the experience characteristic. The sequence of events, then runs as follows.

A searcher samples from a distribution of job offers, paying c and receiving just one offer. the joint distribution function $H(w, u)$ is the probability that a job selected at random offers a wage no greater than w *and* a total utility $(w + s)$ no greater than u.[9] A pair (w, u) completely characterise a job. Initially however, only w is observable, and search is over the marginal distribution of wage offers $F(w)$. It a wage offer is rejected — that is, $w \notin \mathcal{W}$ — then search continues anew next period. If a wage is found such that $w \in \mathcal{W}$ then the job is taken for just one period at the end of which the total value of u is known. If the total value is not acceptable then the worker may quit to search again. A job for which u is acceptable in kept on in perpetuity.

The return to search employing an acceptance set in the current period and employing optimal acceptance sets in the future is:

$$V(\mathcal{W}) = -c + \varrho \int_{\mathcal{W}} Z^*(W)dF(W)$$

$$+ \varrho V^* \left[1 - \int_{\mathcal{W}} dF(W) \right] \qquad (3.39)$$

where $Z^*(w)$ is the maximum return to accepting a wage w. An investigation of $Z^*(w)$ is crucial if we are to establish the form of $\mathcal{W}$. Hence, suppose a value of w has just been accepted, then if $\mathcal{U}$ is the set of acceptable u-values, we have:

$$Z(\mathcal{U}, w) = \int_o^\infty UdG(U \mid w) + \frac{\varrho}{(1-\varrho)} \int_{\mathcal{U}} UdG(U \mid w)$$

$$+ \varrho V^* \left[1 - \int_{\mathcal{U}} dG(U \mid w) \right] \qquad (3.40)$$

The first term is the expected value of u given that a wage w is accepted this is earned just for one period. The second term is the expected value of u given that it is acceptable multiplied by the probability that $u \in \mathcal{U}$ discounted so that it is earned in each successive period. The final term is the maximum return to search multiplied by the probability that the worker quits.

Consider the form of $\mathcal{U}$. If a job is accepted on a permanent basis the worker receives a total of $u/(1-\varrho)$ and a quit has a maximum return of V^*. Given the assumption of infinite horizon, and so on, V^* is a constant, so that the searcher will unambiguously prefer higher u-values. A reservation value of u therefore determines $\mathcal{U}$ and the optimal reservation value satisfies:

$$\frac{u^*}{(1-\varrho)} = V^* \qquad (3.41)$$

The worker's permanent job decision is therefore:

$$\left. \begin{array}{l} \text{Accept the } u\text{-value if} \quad u \geqq u^* \\ \text{Quit and search again if } u < u^* \end{array} \right\} \qquad (3.42)$$

The optimal reservation value of u^* is found by substituting the interval $[u, \infty)$ for $\mathcal{U}$ in (3.40) and using (3.41). We have:

$$Z^*(w) = \int_0^\infty U dG(U \mid w) + \frac{\varrho}{(1-\varrho)} \int_{u*}^\infty (U - u^*) dG(U \mid w)$$

$$+ \frac{\varrho u^*}{(1-\varrho)} \qquad (3.43)$$

Return now to (3.39). Using now familiar arguments, the expected value of accepting an offer w is $Z^*(w)$, while that of rejection is V^*, so that higher wage offers are unambiguously preferred to low offers only if $Z^*(w)$ increases in w. Hence, a reservation wage rule is appropriate, for the initial decision of $Z^*(w)$ is monotonic increasing in w. The reservation wage satisfies $Z^*(r^*) = V^*$ and so if $Z^{*\prime}(w) > o$, we have, at the initial stage;

Accept w if $w \geqslant r^*$

Reject w if $w < r^*$ $\qquad (3.44)$

where $r^* = Z^{*-1}(V^*)$.

Using (3.43), a sufficient condition for $Z^{*\prime}(w) > o$ is $dG(u \mid w)/dw < o$ for all w and u.[10] The meaning of this is illustrated in Figure 3.2. Essentially, the rule (3.44) is optimal if higher wage offers are associated with more favourable distributions of u-values. Technically, the condition is that higher wage offers induce distributions of u which stochastically dominate these distributions of u associated with lower wage offers.

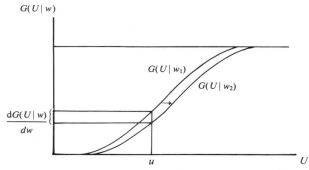

Figure 3.2: First-degree stochastic dominance $(w_2 > w_1)$

The most important comparative–static result is that an increase in the search cost lowers $r*$[11] and lowers the reservation total utility level $u*$ thus lowering the probability that the worker will quit.

3.7   ADAPTIVE SEARCH

One important class of problem avoided so far is that of *adaptive* search. These models set out to capture the idea that the *distribution* of offers is not known for certain so that, as search proceeds, offers received not only have a value as a potential source of income but also as a piece of information about the true wage distribution. In general, the approach to adaptive sequential decision-making can be very complex, and often the additional complexity is not rewarded by additional insights. In view of this I shall simply sketch the key elements of the adaptive search problem.

The fact that the distribution of wage offers is itself unknown requires a technique which relates a searcher's decision to a *subjective* evaluation of the wage-offer distribution. One method of doing this is by use of Bayes' theorem (see Hey, 1981). In essence, this allows current information (in the form of observed wage offers) to be used to update a *prior* evaluation of the distribution.

Let a distribution of offers be completely specified by a vector of paramaters x, and write the distribution function as $F(W|x)$ to reflect this. Further let x be composed of the searcher's subjective assessment of the parameter values so that $F(W|x)$ is the *prior* subjective evaluation of the distribution. Of course, if we allow current information to affect the prior distribution, x will change as an offer is received. To reflect this, an observation w will change the prior evaluation of the parameters from x to $x(w)$, and the (*posterior*) distribution changes to $F(W|x(w))$. The translation from $F(W|x)$ to $F(w|x(w))$ being the result of the application of Bayes' theorem. Hence a current wage offer, whether or not it is acceptable contains information about the distribution.

Suppose we start from the prior position and receive a wage offer w. In the simple search model the choice is one of accepting w, with total value of $w/(1 - \varrho)$ or continue to search in an optimal manner. However, the return to search in the following period will differ, in general, from that associated with the current period because the observation w affects the perceived wage opportunities. Using notation similar to that underlying (3.20), let $\tilde{V}^*(w, x(w))$ be the maximum expected return when an offer w is currently held and the parameter vector is thought to be $x(w)$, then:

$$\tilde{V}^*(w, x(w)) = \varrho \max\left[\frac{w}{(1 - \varrho)}, -c\right.$$

$$\left. + \int_o^\infty \tilde{V}^*(W, x(W))dF(W \mid x(w))\right] \qquad (3.45)$$

where the second term in square brackets — the return to search — may be denoted by V^* in keeping with the earlier notation. Hence, a reservation wage r^* is the unique solution to:

$$r^* = (1 - \varrho)V^* \qquad (3.46)$$

(and $w < (1 - \varrho)V(w, x(w))$ for $w < r^*$).

Unfortunately, a unique solution to (3.46) is not guaranteed, and to see why we make use of Figure 3.3.

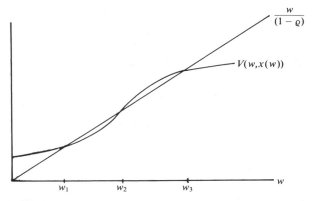

Figure 3.3: Non-uniqueness of the reservation wage under adaptive search

Obviously, the return to future search depends on the current wage offer (and, by implication, on the wage offers received in the past). In Figure 3.3 wages up to w_1 are not acceptable and search continues, while wages between w_1 and w_2 are acceptable. However, the information content of a wage received between w_2 and w_3 is such as to raise the expected return to search. If one of these moderately high wages were received this would be interpreted by the searcher as indicating the potential benefit of continued search. Rejection of high wage offers above w_3 is not optimal as the value of $w > w_3$ as income dominates its values as information.

In general then, little may be said about the outcome of adaptive behaviour, though by assuming particular forms for $F(W \mid x)$ (such as the normal distribution) the form of $F(W \mid x(w))$ and hence $V^*(x(w))$ may be derived using standard techniques. The details involved are out of the scope of this book and the interested reader is referred to Hey (1981) and DeGroot (1970).

3.8   CONCLUSION

This chapter has outlined the more important developments of the simple job-search model.

The use of the recall/no recall distinction is to be found in the early paper by Gronau (1971), and in Kohn and Shavell (1974), while in addition to Burdett (1978) the on-the-job search problem is discussed in Parsons (1973). It is also worth mentioning that the falling reservation wage result of the finite horizon model can be obtained in an infinite horizon model in which either the distribution of offers deteriorates (Lippman and McCall, 1976c) or if per period search costs increase over time (Rice, 1978).

The discussion of expected utility maximisation is incomplete. For example, no mention is made here of utility for consumption, of the budget constraint, or of the work—leisure choice — all of which figure in general microeconomic discussions. I return to contributions which relate to these matters in Chapter 6.

The problem of residual uncertainty and the nature of the

solution has been discussed in Hey (1979b) and McKenna (1979) in addition to Wilde (1979).

The theory of adaptive search behaviour has not really developed fully because, however appealing this work is in its attempt to capture searcher's vagueness about the wage offer distribution, the results usually do not justify the additional complexities. Interested readers are referred to Kohn and Shavell (1974), Rothschild (1974) and Sant (1977).

3.9 EXERCISES

3.1 Consider carefully the model of section 3.3 in which a searcher facing a finite horizon may recall previously rejected offers. Would search ever terminate by the taking-up of any past offer?

3.2 How is the model of section 3.4(i) of Burdett affected by the possibility that in any period individuals face a *fourth* option — that of leaving the market entirely, with constant return V_o?

3.3 In the context of the model of section 3.6, prove the assertion in the text that an increase in the search cost lowers r^* and u^*. What effect does an a change in ϱ have on these variables?

3.4 Using the residual uncertainty model, suppose that, once employed, the searcher faces a probability l of being permanently laid off at the end of the first period. Examine the impact of a change in l on r^* and u^*.

3.5 Again using the model of section 3.6, suppose that the value of s is discovered after n periods rather than after one period. What is the effect of an increase in n on r^* and u^*?

3.6 In labour economics, the theory of compensating wage differentials implies that there is a *negative* association between wage and non-wage characteristics of jobs in competitive equilibrium. In the model of section 3.6 the preservation of the reservation wage rule appears to require a *positive* association. What do you conclude from this?

4 The Firm in an Uncertain Labour Market

4.1 INTRODUCTION

In the context of standard microeconomic theory, the analysis so far has been concerned solely with the supply side of the labour market. The demand side, summarised in the availability of jobs and terms of employment, has been parametric. In the context of the simple job-search model, this amounts to the existence of a known, unchanging and non-degenerate distribution of wage offers, and so the analysis is strictly partial. A model of market equailibrium must explain how a distribution of offers is sustained in a single market. If firms are allowed to make wage adjustments in the light of their market experience, what guarantee is there that eventually all firms will not settle on the same wage offer? Clearly, a coherent discussion of market activity is possible only if wage-setting behaviour of firms is specified. Before making a detailed study, there are some general points to be made.

That each firm is responsible for wage-setting will be a main feature of the discussion of this chapter. At the same time the market studied will be composed of a large number of firms, in whch case we need an explanation of why firms are not individual wage-takers. The brief answer is that the market environment allows firms to hold some monopsony power. In a market of searching workers some wage offers are more likely to be accepted than others, and the firm, by changing its offer, can regulate the rate at which vacancies are filled. If searchers have unique minimum reservation wages, it is higher wages which fill vacancies more quickly and less output is forgone. However, high wages also add to firms' costs, so that the optimal wage offer will be the result of a balance between a desire to fill the vacancy with a productive worker quickly, and a desire to keep down wage costs. The precise conditions under which this type of behaviour takes place constitute the body of sections 4.2 and 4.3.

As with the discussion of workers search the trading arangements are *decentralised*, there is no mystical 'auctioneer', and exchange is a bilateral agreement between a worker and a firm. The consequences of this for the operation of the market as a whole are discussed in section 4.4.

4.2 THE GENERATION OF VACANCIES

The main problem investigated in the literature is how a firm in an uncertain labour market fills a given single vacancy in an optimal way. A prior question, then, is how vacancies may be generated. In the case of a new or expanding firm the answer is obvious. Otherwise, we need to identify the sources of labour *turnover*; that is, to discover reasons why job matches break-up (see Eaton and Watts, 1977, Watts, 1978).

From the previous chapter it is apparent that there are to hand several explanations of voluntary quits by workers. In short, a quit may result either from a worker discovering an improved job offer following a period of on-the-job search, or from a worker being so disattisfied with some aspect of the job that the total job satisfaction falls below a minimum acceptable level. In either case, the firm is left with a vacancy.

In the next section, the optimal job-offer behaviour of a firm will be studied in detail, but we should observe at this point that the terms of the job offer made by a firm are endogenous. This means that a firm experiencing excessive voluntary turnover may be prompted to improve its wage offer or some other job attribute; the firm then realises that is has some control over both the initial flow of applicants *and* the turnover of its workforce.

Some turnover is initiated by employers in the form of dismissals,[1] and a firm finding itself having to dismiss a large number of unsatisfactory workers might look closer at its recruiting policy. Less obvious to classify is the case of induced 'voluntary' turnover. In this case the worker quits, not because of the revalations of some previously unseen disutility, but because the firm *changes* the terms and conditions. A wage cut, for example will, for most firms, induce some quits.

Turnover also results from retirement, death, illness and transitions into non-participation. Retirement may be statutory, but may also result from a utility-maximising decision by a worker for whom continued work is not compensated by the wage, and who therefore places a high value on leisure time. In addition to the immediate consequences of deaths and illnesses, there may also be indirect complications for a firm's turnover experience. In the context of industrial injuries, the safety record of a firm might be an important non-pecuniary job charcteristic. If the safety record is discernible only if a job is accepted, then the worker respons to its revelation in a way suggested in the residual uncertainty model of section 3.6. In this case we must also be aware of the existence of insurance markets for workers and of industrial compensation arrangements. Finally, moves into non-participation may be due to domestic circumstances, but also may be motivated by financial inducement or leisure preference.

(i)   Initial hires
The simplest case to consider is when a new firm is established. The firm has no turnover history and simply seeks to fill each vacancy with a suitable worker at an appropriate wage. The number of vacancies is determined by the production technology and the size of the firm. In a market of searching workers the time to fill each vacancy is random and, in general, will depend on the firm's wage offer and its recruitment policy. If all workers are equally productive the recruitment policy is trivial — any worker attracted by the wage offer is accepted. If workers are not equally productive then the firm must either establish the productivity of an applicant before hire, hire in total ignorance of productivity and make 'adjustments' afterwards, or invest in some information-gathering technique at the time of hire and respond appropriately when actual productivity is perceived.

The last option is the most widely-used method in practice, and largely depends on the existence of signals: easily observed but not totally accurate indicators of likely productivity. Qualifications, references and interview performance, for example, often contribute to a firm's picture of a candidate's ability. In turn, job applicants can 'invest' in signalling devices in order that the most favourable impression possible is made. A literature on this problem has developed, but I shall not enlarge on the issues here.[2]

For reasons of simplicity, differences in worker productivity are usually either ignored (see below, section 4.3), assumed to be fully perceived at the time of hire (Pissarides, 1976a) or assumed to be fully perceived, with no prior screening, by experience (McKenna, 1980). In the last two cases, the problem arises of how the firm should adjust if the wage offer which attracts a worker to a job is not appropriate for the (correctly) perceived productivity. Pissarides (1976a) has identified two classes of response according to the (exogenously determined) flexibility or otherwise of the initial wage offer. A 'flexwage' environment is one in which the firm may revise the wage offer on discovery of a worker's productivity but at the risk of losing the applicant. Because firms are often inhibited from discriminating between workers, wage revisions to suit each worker's productivity may be replaced by a recruitment standard under 'fixwage', the recruitment standard being a predetermined minimum acceptable level of ability, determined not only by technological factors but also by a desire to keep only a moderate wedge between the wage and revenue product. In McKenna (1980) the enforcement of the recruitment standard by the firm results in dismissal.

For a firm facing a group of searchers of uniform ability with different reservation wages and no turnover, the story of its optimal policy ends when all vacancies are filled. The only issue is the wage rate chosen to fill each vacancy. I return to this in section 4.3. For firms experiencing *subsequent* turnover the problem is more involved.

(ii) Voluntary turnover

A firm's wage and employment policy in general should take account of the fact that subsequent quits are likely. If quits are at all costly then the firm will want to make its own job offer relatively more attractive than if no quits took place. this is achieved by raising its wage offer and improving other conditions of work. Both on-the-job search and the resolution of residual uncertainty are less likely to result in quits if the firm follows this policy. It is unlikely however that an attempt to eliminate quits entirely would prove to be profitable.

An important complication is that if firms which differ only in their quit rates offer different wages and other benefits, then in general a firm's job offer will depend on its recent history of voluntary turnover. Since the quit rate is at least in part random, an 'unlucky' firm which has attracted a number of particularly fussy workers will be forced to offer a higher utility package than a 'lucky' firm with a lower quit rate.

Although in practice firms will not vary their working conditions or wages in response to transient changes in the quit rate it is likely that the job offer will reflect to some extent the turnover history. Firms with unusually low job-utility offers will be forced to make improvements or simply accept or tolerate a high quit rate.

(iii) Involuntary turnover

A firm which finds itself having to dismiss large numbers of unsatisfactory workers may choose to invest more resources in candidate selection. To accept a high rate of involuntary separation is to run the risk of acquiring a reputation as an unreliable employer. *Ceteris paribus* these high turnover firms may also need to make higher initial wage offers to compensate workers for bearing the perceived turnover risk. Again then we expect, in general, that the firm's optimal offer and recruitment policy will depend on recent involuntary turnover experience.

These quite general remarks about the sources of vacancies are a useful background to the analysis of this chapter, but a model which takes account of all sources of turnover and a firm's optimal responses to its history is not available. For this reason, we should focus attention on a relatively narrow problem: that of a single firm with a single vacancy.

4.3 THE WAGE OFFER

The simplest case to consider is the demand side counterpart of the simple infinite horizon model of worker search. The firm has a single vacancy which it fills just once at an announced wage rate. Ignoring for the moment the behaviour of a firm's competitors in the labour market, the firm's choice of wage offer will be determined by a desire to keep wage costs to a minimum and a desire to make the wage offer sufficiently attractive that a searcher will find the offer acceptable. To put force behind this latter consideration, suppose that workers use the reservation wage rule (2.5), have different reservation wages, but are otherwise homogeneous. If the distribution function of reservation wages is denoted by $G(r)$, then $G(w)$ is the probability that a worker randomly selecting to search a particular firm will find its wage offer w acceptable. Further, if k is the cost to the firm of having a vacancy open and ϱ the discount factor, then $\pi(w)$, the expected discounted profit from a vacancy offering a wage w, is given by:

$$\pi(w) = -k + \frac{\varrho(x-w)}{(1-\varrho)} G(w) + \varrho\pi^*[1 - G(w)] \qquad (4.1)$$

where an accepted job is taken up at the beginning of the following period, x is the common marginal revenue product of workers,[3] and the firm behaves optimally in the future should the vacancy not be filled in the current period. The infinite horizon constancy of k and the unchanging distribution ensure that $\pi(w)$ is the same in each period. The firm's problem is to choose w so as to maximise (4.1), giving:

$$\pi^* = \frac{(x-w)}{(1-\varrho)} - \frac{G(w)}{(1-\varrho)g(w)} \qquad (4.2)$$

which on substitution into (4.1) gives:

$$\pi^* = -k + \frac{\varrho(x-w)}{(1-\varrho)} - \frac{\varrho G(w)[1 - G(w)]}{(1-\varrho)g(w)} \qquad (4.3)$$

A few remarks are in order here. First, equation (4.2) is by way of an *optimality condition* — the firm should choose its wage offer so as to satisfy (4.2) if it seeks to maximise its net discounted expected profit from having the vacancy. On the other hand, equation (4.3) is an expression for the value of the maximised expected profit level when the wage offer is chosen optimally.

Secondly, it is clear from (4.3) that the choice of w ensures that the discounted profit from a hired worker, $\varrho(x-w)/(1-\varrho)$ more than compensates the firm for the cost of having the vacancy left unfilled for one period; that is, $\varrho(x-w)/(1-\varrho)-k > 0$. This result arises because the firm bears the risk of being unable to fill the vacancy in any single period, and the firm sets its wage offer so that it is rewarded for this risk-bearing when a worker is hired. Hence, in this model, the wage will not equal the worker's marginal revenue product, even though there is no uncertainty surrounding the productivity of a hired worker.

The optimal wage offer made by the firm in this case depends on the distribution of reservation wages, the vacancy cost, the productivity of workers and the discount rate. The increase in the cost to the firms of holding the vacancy k, increases the wage offer made. This is because the firm, wanting to lower the cost of failing to attract the worker, increases the probability of filling the vacancy by increasing its wage offer. An increase in worker productivity similarly increases the wage offer, because the firm is more able to afford to increase the probability of filling the vacancy. The effect of a change is ϱ on w is left as an exercise.

Finally, there are some features of the production process implicit in the model which are worthy of comment. In the explanation of equation (4.1), x is defined as the 'common marginal revenue product of workers'; that is, productivity is thought of as being a worker attribute. Alternatively, in this world of homogeneous workers, it may be regarded as a firm attribute — a feature of the production function — and since, to avoid complications we want x to be independent of the size of the labour force, we are implicitly assuming constant returns to labour. Other assumptions are possible. For example, retaining the labour homogeneity assumption we could made x a decreasing function of the size of the labour force — that is, diminishing returns to labour. In a world of heterogeneous workers, however, not all variations in product will be attributable to the properties of the production function and with random job matches there is a chance that relatively 'inefficient' workers may be hired before relatively efficient workers. This possibility exists, for example, in the model of section 4.4(ii). Only a stochastic marginal product schedule exists *ex ante*.

In an uncertain world it seems appropriate to attribute marginal product variations as reflecting the quality of the job match being neither a purely technological feature of the production function nor a pure index of worker ability or training. For the most part in this chapter the precise source of variations in x are not important. In particular, since we are attempting to abstract from the firm size by considering only additional vacancies there is no necessity to attempt an explanation of systematic variations in marginal products.

As simple as this model is, it has many useful features which I return to in section 4.5. Unfortunately, this simplicity also makes it impossible to study most features of labour market turnover. The only turnover in this model, as with the simple worker search model, is the movement of workers from an unemployed to an employed state. In view of the discussion of section 4.2 there are many more possibilities to be studied.

4.4 WAGE AND EMPLOYMENT ADJUSTMENT

The problem facing the firm changes markedly if searchers have different productive potential, and it is this heterogeneity which makes firms exercise choice between applicants, so far as possible, to employ the most productive workers.

In practice, the process of a firm's selection of its workforce is complex, Initially, the firm has only an impression of the worker's ability drawn from references, qualifications and, perhaps, an interview. This means that in general the firm faces a residual uncertainty about the worker at the time of hire.

A further complication is that productivity is not simply a characteristic of a worker, and it is the quality of the *job match* which produces differences in productivity. Putting the right worker in the right job is a central allocative role for any labour market. The complications do not end here because an identifiable productivity resulting from a particular job match is unlikely to remain unchanged throughout the duration of the employment. Short-run fluctuations may result from changes in the work environment and workers' attitudes, while more durable changes in productivity result from the accumulation of job-specific skills, adjustments in work practices and changes in capital. These issues are too involved to be discussed in detail here and the interested reader is referred to Joll *et al*. (1983) for further treatment. Even so, these complications must be borne in mind when interpreting the results of the models of this chapter.

Towards the end of chapter 2 we met the job-search model of Mortensen (1970), in which a wage offer is related to the productivity requirements of a particular firm. However, a fuller account of the relationship between wages and productivity is required because productivity requirements may be determined by economic factors rather than technology, and because firms may seek to adjust wages in line with an observed productivity.

In what follows, it is convenient to assume that productivity is, in principle, quantifiable and constant for each worker. In particular there will be no potential for the firm to *induce* greater output by incentives, nor will there be other opportunities for productivity improvements.

Consider a firm facing a heterogeneous group of searchers. If the firm knows the distribution of productivities across workers, then a wage-offer calculation will involve not only the probability of acceptance (as in the model of 4.3) but also the expected productivity of the applicant. In general, of course, the actual productivity of an applicant will differ from that expected, and when productivity is observed, the firm may want to revise its contractual terms — particularly if the firm is 'disappointed'. I consider two ways in which firms may respond to a particular productivity outcome.

(i) Wage adjustment
In practice, firms face many constraints on their ability to

invoke a (downward) wage revision in line with productivity. The 'institutional' constraints arise from trade union agreements, and established practice, such as the comparable pay for comparable jobs principle. However, an important economic constraint is the possibility that a downward wage revision will induce the applicant to reject the job after all and search once more, leaving the firm with a vacancy.

This problem raises many interesting possibilities. For example, the firm may be able to calculate the probability that the worker will quit, especially if the realised productivity contains some information about the worker's reservation wage. In the extreme, if the productivity outcome allows the firm to compute *exactly* the worker's reservation wage then the firm's policy is clear since the worker will tolerate any wage reduction as long as the final offer is no less than the reservation wage. The firm will set its offer equal to the reservation wage. In less extreme cases the extent of downward wage revision, where it is warranted, will be moderated by uncertainty about the worker's 'loyalty'.

Another issue relates to the timing of the firm's observation of the worker's productivity. In Pissarides (1976a) the firm observes and takes action on realised productivity immediately an applicant arrives. In this case, the firm does not announce its wage offer until the productivity of the applicant is observed. However, it is more reasonable to think of productivity as an 'experience characteristic', in the sense that it can only be observed with any confidence once the worker is employed. In this case the firm must accept a worker even when there is some residual uncertainty about productivity. For a time the wage paid to the worker will be 'inappropriate' in that it does not relate in any predetermined way to the worker's productivity, and the longer is this trial (or 'observation') period the more costly is any shortfall of productivity. On the other hand, from the worker's viewpoint, this period may constitute an opportunity to reap the unexpected rewards of the employer's uncertainty!

The central question of interest in this model is the following. In the absence of any institutional constraints, how should the firm revise its wage offer when productivity has been realised? The answer depends on the sensitivity of the worker to wage adjustment, and the sensitivity of the firm to turnover. A simple illustration will serve to highlight some of the issues.

Consider a worker endowed with a fixed productivity x. Let $V(x)$ be the maximal return to search and $R(x, w)$ be the *expected* return to accepting a job paying a rate w for this worker. That $R(x, w)$ is an *expected* return results from the fact that some uncertainty remains about the *permanent* contractual conditions even though the initial wage offer is known. This residual uncertainty is caused by possible future wage adjustment by the firm and by the existence of other, as yet unobserved, job characteristics in the spirit of section 3.6. Now, the wage w will be accepted by the worker if $V(x) \leqslant R(x, w)$ in which case the job is taken and (eventually) the previously unobserved contractual terms are revealed.

The firm, on the other hand, is uncertain about a particular worker's productivity since all workers have different x-values which are not so readily observed. The initial wage offer w, therefore, is based on the firm's *expectation* of x Wage revision, and hence the permanent contractual terms offered to the worker, depends on the realised value of x. Two cases appear to be of particular interest. In the first, the realised productivity is lower than that expected by the firm, and the firm will be tempted to lower its wage offer so that it is more in line with productivity. Along similar lines to the model of section 4.3 the revised wage offer, say w_x, may or may not continue to make the permanent job offer preferable to search from the worker's point of view. If it is still true for the worker that $V(x) \leqslant R(x, w_x)$ then the firm will succeed in lowering the wage offer. In general, however, the firm will not be certain that a particular wage reduction will maintain $R(x, w_x)$ above $V(x)$. Intuitively, we would expect the firm to be less willing to take the chance of a large wage reduction if its own turnover costs are high. However, some attempt at wage reduction is likely in this case.

The second, and perhaps more interesting case, is that in which the realised value of x is greater than that expected by the firm and greater than the wage offer. In this case, it is still possible that the firm will find it optimal to lower the wage offer, because it is by no means certain to induce a quit. On the other hand, the firm is less willing to cause the departure of a highly productive worker, and in addition the firm runs the risk that other job characteristics do not meet with the worker's minimum requirements in which case a quit is even more likely. Indeed, it is not unreasonable that a highly productive worker may be rewarded with a wage *increase* as the firm tries to affect the turnover risk caused by the worker being dissatisfied with the total job package. The risk of losing a very productive worker leads the firm to compensate by awarding a wage increase. In other words, if *x* exceeds the firm's expectations, a reduction, increase or no change in the wage are all possible depending on exactly how productive a worker is.

A firm's wage adjustment policy is clearly constrained by the turnover risk which it regards as more serious (in terms of forgone output) the more productive is the worker. In practice, firms are simply unable to make downward wage adjustments because of union resistance, while wage increases to reward productive workers have implications for the entire internal wage structure of the firm. In either event, there is a case for discovering an alternative way in which firms can adjust to realised productivity outcomes.

(ii) Employment adjustment

Assume that, once set, a wage offer made by a firm cannot be changed; that is, the wage offer perceived by a searching worker is certain not to change once the job is taken. Of course, initially the wage offer may be a decision variable of the firm but, once chosen, it is unalterable. In this case, the firm will find an alternative way of discriminating amongst applicants.

Two possibilities suggest themselves. In the first the firm, anxious to avoid making a costly mistake by hiring an unsatisfactory worker, may devote more resources to *screening* job applicants and taking greater care in the initial hiring stage. In the second, the firm may remain relatively unconcerned initially about the quality of the worker hired on the grounds that information gathered by screening is costly and inaccurate. The assessment of a worker's productivity is then carried out in the period immediately following the hire and workers found to be unsatisfactory in some sense are subsequently dismissed. These two methods are often combined in practice, with firms devoting some resources to the initial screening process and some to on-the-job monitoring. Typically, some emphasis is on the former if the firm intends to invest in the worker by intensive training and if dismissal is costly or difficult. On the other hand, firms recruiting unskilled or casual labour have little to gain from costly screening and 'mistakes' are more easily rectified by dismissal.

An underlying concept in either selection method is that of a minimally acceptable performance standard, and it is possible to model this notion in a straightforward way.

Suppose the firm believes that workers' per period outputs x are distributed according to the distribution function $F(x)$, and suppose also that the per period wage rate is fixed at a predetermined level, then, in the spirit of the model of section 4.3, the expected discounted profit from vacancy offering wage w but requiring a minimum per period output of y is:

$$\pi(y) = -k + \frac{\varrho}{(1-\varrho)} \int_y^\infty (x-w)dF(x) + \varrho\pi^*F(y) \quad (4.4)$$

Equation (4.4) reflects the fact that only workers with $x \gtrless y$ are accepted into employment, others being dismissed leaving the firm with π^* once more. Clearly, the optimal value of y satisfies:

$$\pi^* = \frac{(y^* - w)}{(1-\varrho)} \quad (4.5)$$

so that the firm is indifferent between receiving $y^* - w$ profit in each period in perpetuity and receiving π^* by advertising the vacancy once more. Using (4.5) and (4.4), π^* is given by:

$$\pi^* = -k + \frac{\varrho}{(1-\varrho)} \int_{y^*}^\infty (x-y^*)dF(x) + \frac{\varrho(y^* - w)}{(1-\varrho)} \quad (4.6)$$

A simple comparative–static exercise (which is left to the reader) establishes that an increase in the cost of holding the vacancy k makes the firm less choosy about the productivity of the worker by lowering the minimum recruitment standard y^*, while an increase in the wage offer raises y^*, making the firm more anxious to hire a high-productivity worker.

If the worker's productivity can be observed only after one period of employment, equation 4.4 becomes;

$$\pi(y) = -k + \varrho \int_o^\infty (x - w)dF(x) +$$

$$\frac{\varrho}{(1 - \varrho)} \int_y^\infty (x - w)dF(x) + \varrho^2 \pi^* F(y) \qquad (4.7)$$

in which case the optimal policy still requires (4.5) to be satisfied. More importantly, $F(y)$, which previously had the interpretation of being the probability than an applicant is turned away, is now properly interpreted as the probability that a worker is dismissed. This therefore constitutes a model of involuntary or firm-initiated turnover.

A model along these lines is a natural conterpart to the residual uncertainty model of job search outlined in section 3.6. In practice, both workers and firms need time to evaluate the quality of the job match, and this discovery may lead to voluntary quits, involuntary dismissals or an agreement not to proceed beyond a probationary period. A fixed probationary period is a common feature of many job contracts, particularly those involving high levels of skill and training, and is a convenient way of reducing uncertainty about labour turnover. By agreeing that contrast option will only be revised after a particular time, uncertainties arising out of the differences in 'reaction' times of agents are reduced, if not eliminated. In contracts which specify no probationary period, jobs may be terminated by either side as soon as enough information emerges about the quality of the match.

The full implications of invoking a minimum recruitment standard are discussed in McKenna (1980) and Pissarides (1976a), the former incorporating an exogenous probationary period.

If it is not apparent already, it is important to realise that exactly why, apart from institutional considerations, a firm chooses between a 'flexwage' response and one which involves quantity adjustment has not been investigated in the job-search literature. Indeed this question is at the heart of recent discussions of the ways in which economies adjust (Okun, 1981). There is a view that wage inflexibility arises purely from institutional rigidities or 'irrational' behaviour, while much research in the 'implicit contracts' literature in particular (see Hart, 1983, for a recent survey) has shown otherwise. The incorporation of job search into the implicit contract framework (and vice versa) may or may not produce useful insights, but more work on the endogeneity of the wage adjustment decision in a job search theory is now essential.[4]

Identifying demand side counterparts to the various worker search models is on its own a natural enough quest, but it is also forced upon us by the need to complete the market picture.

4.5 MARKET IMPLICATIONS

That such an apparently all-embracing subject as market implications should occupy only a section of a chapter is easily explained. The study of search market equilibrium has proven to be a most difficult problem, and yet it is essential for the credence of the theory that the overall operation of the market should be analysed. In this section I outline the advances that have been made in this area.

We have known for some time that markets with imperfect information and uncoordinated exchange behave in rather different ways to the static certainty models which pervade the economics literature (Arrow, 1959; Rothschild, 1973). For example, in the context of consumer search in an atomistic market composed of identical searchers and firms, price disperion disappears but the limiting price is not necessarily the competitive equilibrium price (Fisher, 1970, 1973; Diamond, 1971; Hey, 1974).

The implications of the degeneracy of the offer distribution for search markets are obvious enough. The search problem as such disappears, though the problem of *finding* a job may remain. A literature on equilibrium price dispersion in consumer search models has now established that, with rational expectations and well-behaved adjustant processes, dispersion is sustained by an equilibrium only if there is some heterogeneity between agents. In Reinganum (1979) and McMinn (1980a) firms differ in production costs, while in Axell (1974), Salop and Stiglitz (1977) and Carlson and McAfee (1983) consumer search costs differ. In Butters (1977) price differences result from different advertising policies of firms, while in Burdett and Judd (1983) they result from (random) differences in the amount of information collected by searchers. In Ionnides (1975) price dispersion results from continual arrival of new entrants and departure of old participants. These consumer search models have analogies in the labour market context, and it is on these that attention is focused here.

The type of equilibrium most often studied is whether, and under what circumstances, a non-degenerate distribution of wage offers will result from the optimal decisions of agents on both sides of the market. In this case trades do not actually take place so that questions of labour market flows do not arise.

Alternatively, equilibrium may be seen as the stability of a process taking place through time in which matches are made, firms and workers enter and leave the market, and matches break up. I shall offer some general remarks on this difficult equilibrium issue later.

In a market composed of large numbers infinitely-lived identical workers and firms, the wage offer distribution collapses to a single wage as long as wage-adjustment procedures used by firms are regular (exercise 4.6). In looking for non-trivial solutions to the search equilibrium it is necessary to identify sources of heterogeneity between workers. At the least we require a distribution of reservation wages over workers to support a distribution of wage offers.

In the context of sequential search equilibrium it appears that heterogeneity on each side of the market will generate equilibrium distributions. For example, MacMinn (1980b) has produced an equilibrium wage distribution for the case in which workers differ in search costs and firms differ in production costs. The mechanics involved in this type of analysis are best illustrated by an example. The procedure is to find optimal wage offers made by firms for a *given* distribution of reservation wages and a particular cost. Then, taking as parametric a distribution of costs across firms, a distribution of wage offers is induced. Using a model of optimal sequential search the reservation wage for each individual is calculated given the distribution of wage offers and a search cost. A distribution of search costs is then specified across searchers generating a distribution of reservation wages. If the resulting distribution of reservation wages is the same as the one initially assumed to be used by firms in wage-setting, then the entire set of distributions is mutually consistent.

In the following solution strategy I shall specify distributions of reservation wages and wage offers, and then deduce the underlying distributions of costs which makes the entire set of distributions consistent. Furthermore, in constructing an example, one-parameter distributions are preferred for simplicity.

The models of individual behaviour used here are the simplest possible, equation (1.5) for reservation wage determination rewritten here as:

$$c = \int_r^\infty (w - r)dF(W) \tag{4.8}$$

and equations (4.2) and (4.3) for the case where the discount rate is ignored determine the wage offer for a given vacancy cost:

$$k = \frac{[G(w)]^2}{g(w)} \tag{4.9}$$

We know also that $dr/dc < 0$ and $dw/dk < 0$, and we shall be able to verify these results presently, in the context of our specific example.

I shall assume that searchers are large in number and differ only in their search costs. The relationship between search costs and the reservation wage is clearly one-to-one, so that a distribution of search costs induces a distribution of reservation wages through the fact that:[5]

$$g(r) = h(c)\left|\frac{dc}{dr}\right| \tag{4.10}$$

where $g(r)$ and $h(c)$ are the density functions of reservation wages and search costs, respectively.

I shall assume that firms differ in terms of their *vacancy* costs. Since the relationship between the optimal wage offer and vacancy cost is one-to-one a distribution of wage offers is induced by:

$$f(w) = m(k) \left| \frac{dk}{dw} \right| \qquad (4.11)$$

where $f(w)$ and $m(k)$ are the densities of wage offer and vacancy cost distributions, respectively.

To derive explicit solutions for a mutually compatible set of distributions $f(w)$, $g(r)$, $h(c)$, $m(k)$ I shall assume forms for the first two, and derive the forms of $h(c)$ and $m(k)$ necessary to support these.

Hence, assume that $f(w)$ takes the exponential form:

$$f(w) = \begin{cases} \dfrac{e^{-w/a}}{a} & w > 0 \\ o & \text{otherwise} \end{cases} \qquad (4.12)$$

then using (4.8), we have:

$$c = ae^{-r/a} \qquad (4.13)$$

and since $w \in (0, \infty)$, then $r \in (0, \infty)$ so that $c \in (0, a)$. As c approaches zero (a) r approaches infinity (zero). Now:

$$\frac{dc}{dr} = e^{-r/a} \qquad (4.14)$$

and from (4.13):

$$r = -a \, ln\left(\frac{c}{a}\right) \qquad (4.15)$$

Similarly, suppose that $g(r)$ takes the exponential form with parameter b;

$$g(r) = \begin{cases} \dfrac{e^{-r/b}}{b} & r > 0 \\ o & \text{otherwise} \end{cases} \qquad (4.16)$$

then using (4.9), we have:

$$k = b(e^{w/b} + e^{-w/b}) - wb \tag{4.17}$$

or, since $\cosh(x) = (e^x + e^{-x})/2$:

$$k = 2b \cosh\left(\frac{w}{b}\right) - 2b \tag{4.18}$$

Now, $w \in (0, \infty)$, and so $k \in (0, \infty)$ such that w approaches zero (infinity) as k approaches xero (infinity), and further:

$$\frac{dk}{dw} = \frac{\sinh\left(\frac{w}{b}\right)}{b} \tag{4.19}$$

with (from (4.18)):[6]

$$w = b \cosh^{-1}\left(\frac{k + 2b}{2b}\right)$$

$$= b \, ln\left(\frac{k + 2b}{2b}\right) \tag{4.20}$$

We are now in a position to derive the underlying distributions of $h(c)$ and $m(k)$ responsible for generating the distributions (4.12) and (4.16).

First, using (4.14) (4.15) and (4.16) in (4.1), we have:

$$h(c) = \begin{cases} \dfrac{\left(\dfrac{a}{c}\right)^{(b-a)/b}}{b} & c \in (0, a), \ b \geqslant \frac{1}{2} \\ o & \text{otherwise} \end{cases} \tag{4.21}$$

Similarly, using (4.12) (4.18) and (4.19) in (4.11) we have:

$$m(k) = \begin{cases} \dfrac{b \exp\left[-\dfrac{b}{a} ln\dfrac{(k + 2b)}{2b}\right]}{a \, \sinh\left(ln\left(\dfrac{k + 2b}{2b}\right)\right)} & k > 0, \ b \geqslant \frac{1}{2} \\ o & \text{otherwise} \end{cases}$$

or, using the fact that $\sinh(\ln x) = x$:

$$m(k) = \begin{cases} \dfrac{b}{a}\left(\dfrac{k+2b}{2b}\right)^{-(a+b)/a} & k > 0, b \geqslant \tfrac{1}{2} \\ 0 & \text{otherwise} \end{cases} \qquad (4.22)$$

To summarise, the example suggests that given wage-setting by firms and reservation wage-setting by workers, but allowing no contract to be formed, the (exponential) distributions of wage offers and reservation wage offers given by (4.12) and (4.16) are equilibrium distributions with respect to the underlying distributions of costs given by (4.21) and (4.22). A more general treatment along similar lines may be found in MacMinn (1980b).

In general, sustained wage dispersion requires some form of heterogeneity or additional sources of randomness which affect wage offer and reservation wage decisions. For example, in Pissarides (1976a) the finite horizon nature of the model makes reservation wages and wage offers time-dependent — if individuals join the market at different times, distributions are sustained because of differences in the duration of market activity. In a non-sequential formulation, Wilde (1977) establishes a non-degenerate distribution of wage offers by introducing a stochastic element into the number of offers a worker may receive in each period. Since workers will choose a maximum of a set of offers received, and since the (expected) maximum depends on the number of offers, firms can successfully hire workers by making *different* wage offers because workers will be faced with different sample sizes. Firms offering the lowest wage, for example, can still attract labour because of the possibility that this wage will be the 'best' offer received by a worker who only draws one wage. Thus an *ex post* heterogeneity is induced across workers by the realisation of the (random) number of offers resulting from a single search trial.

Once equilibrium distributions are established, matches can be made and that, as far as the models under discussion here are concerned, is the end of the story. In the absence of a predetermined number of vacancies in each firm, the resulting distribution of the size of firms is also then an equilibrium. Furthermore, if each firm makes zero profits in equilibrium, then given a fixed workforce the number of firms in the market may also be determined.

The issue of the market solution is considerably more involved if matches are allowed to take place out of equilibrium. The way in which search markets established on equilibrium when job matches break up has been studied using computer simulations by Eaton and Watts (1977). In their model adjustment occurs because workers have incomplete knowledge of the distribution of wage offers. Models which allow job matches to be made must additionally specify how matches break up, how wage adjustments are made, and must model 'births' and 'deaths' so that the market does not 'dry up' as a fixed pool of unemployed eventually find jobs.

Models which allow for heterogeneity in productivity face additional complexities. The market in this case is composed of workers with broadly similar skills but who have different and possibly uncertain productivities. Differences in productive performance may be due to subtle differences in ability or luck in finding a suitable working environment. Once the market is defined the equilibrium methods outlined in this section are, in principle, applicable to the residual uncertainty model, though in practice an analytical solution has to be accomplished.

4.6 CONCLUSION

It is clear from the discussion in this chapter that the most challenging areas of research and those least developed are on the labour demand and market equilibrium issues. The determinants of the size and number of firms in the market along with how firms choose between wage and 'quantity' adjustment are in need of much further work.

The problem of market equilibrium lies in its complexity, with all but the simple models defying analytical solutions. However, simple equilibrium models of job matching take us some way in understanding the properties of search markets. In Chapter 6 such a model is discussed in the context of allocative efficiency; while in Chapter 7 some insights into the determinants of unemployment are also obtained.

4.7 EXERCISES

4.1 Prove the statements in the text of section 4.3 that the firm's wage offer increases the more costly is the holding of a vacancy and the more productive are workers. What is the effect of a change in the firm's discount rate on the wage offer?

4.2 Using the model of section 4.3, suppose the firm faces a known probability q that the worker will quit after one period in the job. (If the worker does not quit after one period the worker stays on forever.) Examine the consequences of an increase in the quit probability for the firm's wage offer. Establish whether the wage offered in the presence of a turnover risk exceeds, equals or falls short of the wage offered in the absence of a turnover risk.

4.3 In section 4.4(i) the firm's wage adjustment policy is discussed for the case in which actual productivity of a hired worker is lower than expected, and the case in which it is higher than expected. What do you think the firm will do if the realised productivity is exactly what the firm expected it to be?

4.4 Prove the statements in the text of section 4.4(i) that the firm employs a stricter recruitment policy the lower is the cost of holding a vacancy and the higher is the (predetermined) wage offer.

4.5 Using the model of equation (4.7) introduce the additional assumption that if a worker is dismissed (with probability $F(y)$) then the firm incurs a turnover (severance) cost of t — a known lump-sum. Calculate the effect of an increase in t on the firm's recruitment standard and hence on firm-initiated turnover.

4.6 Provide an argument to justify the claim in the text that, for an arbitrary initial distribution of wage offers and identical workers, the equilibrium wage distribution is degenerate. What assumption must be made about the wage-adjusted mechanism made by firms?

5 Empirical Implications

5.1 INTRODUCTION

The empirical work on job-search models is contained in relatively few sources and does not match the theoretical literature in scope or variety. The reason is largely a paucity of suitable data, but also there are difficulties in applying standard econometric techniques to intercept the data. In consequence only those hypotheses derived from the simplest search models have attracted attention, and even here data *and* the econometrics have been stretched.

The data problem relates to the need for individual labour market histories and characteristics to be documented. Aggregate labour market data conceal too much information to be useful in allowing a job-search interpretation. It has been clear for some time that 'panel data' or 'longitudinal data' offer the only satisfactory statistical sources, but even here the interpretation of, and the statistical procedures used to summarise, the information both need great care.

The need for quite detailed information is best illustrated by an example. Consider a test of the hypothesis that the reservation wage declines as (search) unemployment continues because of the finite horizon faced by the searcher. Now, other difficulties apart, the finding of evidence of falling reservation wages among a group of unemployed workers may be attributed to increasing search costs, learning, increasing impatience, wealth depletion or the finite horizon. Quite often we find that the general hypothesis of a falling reservation wage may be supported, but that the data do not contain sufficient information to enable us to distinguish between the specific hypotheses.

The empirical literature has developed over the past fifteen

84

years, but only recently have problems of interpreting panel data been met directly by econometricians. The econometric issues are in detail rather complex, but two difficulties are the interpretation of duration data and the modelling of the stochastic (uncertain) environment. In many studies there is the additional problem of unobservability both of individual characteristics and of a key concept in search theory — the reservation wage.

The relatively recent developments in econometric methods for seach models divide the empirical literature into two groups. In the earlier work the data were analysed primarily by the estimation of regression equations by ordinary least squares and the econometric difficulties this creates, though often recognised, were side-stepped. After discussing the hypotheses of search models in section 4.2 I outline the various findings reported in these earlier studies. In section 5.3 I examine the recent econometric work on search models: the key empirical findings relating to the duration of unemployment and reservation wages are summarised in the conclusion.

5.2 THE HYPOTHESES AND EARLY RESULTS

Most of the empirical job-search literature has been concerned with the implication of reservation wage behaviour for the duration of unemployment spells, though subsidiary hypotheses about participation, post-search earnings and the effects of changes in the search environment on behaviour have also been investigated.

(i) Duration of unemployment and reservation wage determination

For most studies, the key relationship is that between the reservation wage and the probability of leaving unemployment or, alternatively, the expected duration of unemployment. Recall that for an unemployed searcher with reservation wage r the probability that a job is accepted in any period (and hence that unemployment ends) is:

$$p = [1 - F(r)] \tag{5.1}$$

while the expected duration of the unemployment spell is $1/p$. This, of course, is a relationship derived from the simplest of the sequential search models, in which only the search cost, wage-offer distribution and possibly a discount factor determine the reservation wage and hence the duration of unemployment. In practice, and in more general models, the reservation wage is determined by many more parameters, including the arrival time of offers, attitudes to risk, moving costs, past experiences, human capital, age and other personal characteristics. Any of these, or any combination of these, may account for differences in individuals' reservation wages and hence account for differences in individuals' expected duration of unemployment spells.

Several studies have attempted to account for differences in individuals' reservation wages, and duration of unemployment. In these studies it is interesting to note how various theoretical concepts are measured in practice.

In a study by Feinberg (1977b), search costs are measured in terms of travel costs and unemployment benefits; the former have a negative effect on unemployment duration, and the latter a positive effect. the use of unemployment insurance or unemployment benefit to capture (negative) search costs is very common. Chapin (1971) finds that the ratio of unemployment benefit to wage[1] in last job increases the duration of unemployment. Similarly, Ehrenberg and Oaxaca (1976) find that a higher unemployment insurance increases the duration of unemployment of young workers. Older workers it seems are more likely to *intensify* their search activity rather than prolong it when the search subsidy is higher. The theory underlying the role of unemployment benefits in search models goes beyond its use as a search subsidy however, and I consider this again in the next chapter.

When duration of unemployment data are available it is natural to seek direct effects of parameter changes on duration. In terms of equation (5.1) however, this is taking a back-door approach, avoiding entirely the reservation wage concept. Panel data quite often contain questions which can be taken as enquiries about reservation wages, although the phrasing of the question is crucial if the response is to have the reservation wage interpretation. Something along the lines of 'What is the *lowest* amount per week you are prepared to accept in a new job?' comes as close as any question to an enquiry about a reservation wage.[2] The answer to such a question allowed Feinberg (1978b)[3] to estimate a reservation wage equation using a measure of search costs, risk aversion (studied also in Feinberg, 1977b) and distributional parameters; namely, the mean and standard deviation of the wage-offer distribution. Individuals with higher search costs and greater risk-aversion are found to have lower reservation wages, while those facing distributions with larger means and larger standard deviations are found to have larger reservation wages. This last result is particularly interesting. In general, reservation wages are positively related to the return to search, and it is apparent from Feinberg's study that a greater dispersion of wage offers is regarded as an increase in the return to search, although this is unlikely to be the case for individuals who are highly risk-averse.

The return to search is determined both by the potential wage gains *and* employment opportunities. After all, being in a market with some potentially very high wage offers is of little comfort if jobs are relatively scarce, hence the rate at which vacancies can be discovered or the arrival rate of offers affects the reservation wage, as we saw in exercise 2.3. The theoretical basis for this, as well as initial empirical work, is due to Barron (1975). The intuition is relatively straightforward. In a 'tight' labour market, where vacancies are few and unemployment high, the probability of finding a vacancy is low and hence the returns to search are low. Alternatively, the returns to search are *pro-cyclical*.

Barron (1975) identifies three ways in which the vacancy rate affects the duration of unemployment. In the first, and the most direct, a fall in the vacancy rate makes a job contact less likely and *ceteris paribus* prolongs the expected duration of unemployment. In the second, this direct effect is counteracted by a downward revision of the reservation wage in the light of lower returns to search, thus lowering the expected duration. In the third, a lower vacancy rate may, in a general cyclical downswing, be accompanied by lower wage offers so that the wage distribution shifts to the left. If this shift is not perceived (and so reservation wages are not adjusted) searchers will find fewer jobs acceptable and the expected duration of unemployment increases. In fact, Barron finds the first effect dominant so that a lower vacancy rate tends to increase duration. Axelsson and Löfgren (1977) find a similar effect using Swedish data, while Chapin (1971) placed an equivalent interpretation on the finding that an increase in the unemployment rate increases duration, since a higher unemployment rate reduces the chances of any one individual being made an offer.

A more detailed theoretical analysis of cyclical behaviour and job search models must wait until Chapter 7.

(ii) Reservation wage behaviour

The simple search model of Chapter 2 unambiguously predicts that, in a stable environment, the reservation wage of an individual remains constant throughout the duration of unemployment. This prediction is contradicted by several alternative formulations of the job-search problem and, it appears, by the available empirical evidence.

Three alternative formulations of the job-search problem will produce a declining reservation wage over time.[4] The finite horizon model without recall (Gronau, 1971) discussed in Chapter 3 clearly predicts a *monotonic* reduction in the reservation wage over time.

Alternatively, if search is *systematic* rather than random (Salop, 1973) then, since the 'best' firms are approached first, workers become correspondingly less choosy with unsuccessful search, lowering the reservation wage.

Finally, if searchers do not hold rigid subjective views about the wage offer revision but behave adaptively, then the reservation wage[5] will vary as the subjective distribution of wage offers varies. If an individual starts the unemployment spell with a very favourable view of wage opportunities and becomes less optimistic as unemployment continues, then the returns to search and the associated reservation wage will fall.

All empirical studies reject the constant reservation wage hypothesis, though there is considerable variation in estimates of the precise ways in which reservation wages change and the extent of changes. Kasper (1967), and the recent studies to be discussed in the next section, find support for the declining reservation wage. However, Barnes (1975), Melnik and Saks (1977) and Sant (1977) claim that variations in reservation wages are due to adaptive behaviour by searchers in the light of new information. Interestingly, Sant's evidence does not point to a well-behaved monotonic decline in the reservation wage but to a spasmodic downward trend. Thus, to the extent that subjective distributions converge to the 'true' distribution from 'above' they do so only in an irregular way.

The implication of most studies, then, is that the probability of leaving unemployment given by equation (5.1) increases with the duration of the unemployment spell. However, these studies in the main have not tackled the serious difficulties of interpreting the duration data, and since some important issues are involved I shall give a separate treatment of the recent developments in this area in section 5.3.

(iii) Participation
In two papers Feinberg (1975, 1978c) has studied the impact of search variables on the participation decision. Participation is shown to depend negatively on search costs and the degree of risk-aversion, but positively on the mean and standard deviation of the wage-offer distribution. All of these results accord with expectations in view of our earlier discussion on the duration of unemployment.

(iv) Turnover
The main theoretical contribution of the job-search theory here is in explaining voluntary turnover in the form of quits. The theoretical job-search models support two views on the motives for quitting. In the first, quits are the result of successful on-the-job search for a preferred job. In the second, quits result from a dissatisfaction with the present job. The evidence is strongly in favour of the first of these, according to the results in Mattila (1974) Barron and McCafferty (1977) and Black (1980). The overall impression is that dissatisfaction with the current job is not likely to prompt such extreme

behaviour as quitting, but may be sufficient to initiate on-the-job search.

In the US in particular some labour contracts include a lay-off clause which allows firms to initiate temporary lay-offs when demand drops. The laid-off workforce is 'tied in' to the firm awaiting re-hire. However, Bradshaw and Scholl (1976) have produced evidence that, rather than behave in a purely passive way, laid-off workers are quite likely to be engaged in substantial amounts of search for alternative employment.

(v)   Earnings dispersion and gains from search

The gains from search and hence the motivation for search activity are contained in the dispersion of the wage-offer distribution. Some studies have attempted to measure the potential gains from search in particular markets. Of course, one of the presumptions of simple search models is that the markets are composed of identical workers looking for identical jobs, so that wage dispersion is purely the result of uncertainty, whereas in observed labour markets wage dispersion may exist largely if not exclusively because of differences in job and workers characteristics.

Metcalf (1973) has attempted to eliminate the systematic components of wage dispersion in the academic labour market due to differences in qualifications, location, subject, and so on. Any residual or 'unexplained' variation in wages will then reflect the pure gains from search.[6] Following Holtman (1969), and using results from the fixed sample size rule of Stigler (1962), the amount of residual wage dispersion is found to be relatively small. For example, the implied marginal gains for the fourth search for a university post in economics was estimated at 9.2 per cent of mean annual salary (at the time around £1495).

One difficulty of identifying the gains from search is discussed by Mayhew (1977) who examines both inter-plant wage dispersion and *intra-plant* dispersion in a sample of manufacturing labour markets. Wage dispersion within a plant is important, it is argued, because initial wages taken after a period of search do not represent the true gains from search; these are given by the opportunities offered by the entire wage structure within a company. In finding evidence of significanct intra-plant wage dispersion Mayhew infers that since this creates uncertainty about the true earnings potential associated with any initial wage offer the returns to search are thereby reduced. Again, the conclusion is of fairly modest returns to search.

5.3   RECENT DEVELOPMENTS

With some justification the principal focus of interest of recent empirical job-search models is on the implications for the duration of unemployment. Perhaps it might be more correct to say that most recent studies of the duration of unemployment have found the job-search theory a useful analytical framework. Before discussing the results of these recent studies some important issues which arise are discussed in detail since many of the recent studies have involved significant methodological advances.

(i)   Duration data
The key problem with duration data is that only some of the durations recorded by survey will be *completed* spells,[7] and for many respondents, those who are still unemployed, only the duration of unemployment to date can be reported. Clearly for any individual, given the hypothesised random arrival of job offers and the acceptability of only some of these, the actual duration of a spell continuing at the time of a survey is a random variable. For the researcher looking *across* the sample, durations will also differ between individuals because of differences in characteristics and in market experiences. Using (4.1), any differences in the reservation wage r (in general due to differences in search costs, age, family circumstances skills, and so on) will generate different expected durations of unemployment between individuals.

The work of Salant (1977) shows, amongst other things, why it is inappropriate to avoid the problems of uncompleted spells by eliminating these cases and focusing only on the sub-sample of completed spells. The issue is simply that the sub-sample of completed spells is unlikely to be representative of the entire sample. On a first thought it might appear as though a survey occurring during a spell will do so, on average, when the spell is halfway through. Letting D denote the random variable completed duration and T the random variable duration to date of an uncompleted spell, then we might expect:

$$E[T] = \tfrac{1}{2}E[D]$$

across the sample. this would make the computation of the bias quite easy. However, if completed spells of unemployment vary widely in terms of their duration then it is apparent that longer spells are more likely to be captured by the survey than shorter spells; a phenomenon known as 'length-bias'. In general, the relationship between the mean of T across the sample and the mean of D in the population is:[8]

$$\frac{E[T]}{E[D]} = \frac{1}{2}\left(\frac{\text{Var}[D]}{E^2[S]} + 1\right)$$

Hence any study which isolates either sub-sample of recently completed spells only or uncompleted spells only is going to run into sample selection problems. This is critical because if it is systematic, differences in workers which account for differences in duration and if $\text{Var}[D]$ is large then not only is length-bias a feature[9] of the uncompleted spells, but ignoring uncompleted spells implicitly involves systematic exclusion of certain types of individual (those with high reservation wages) from the sample. As Kiefer and Neumann (1979b) and others have discovered, using the implication (from search theory) that certain types of individuals (those with high reservation wages) have on average longer durations and are more likely to figure in a cross-section sample makes uncompleted spells informative and not merely a nuisance.

Indeed, the whole thrust of recent work is to make use of the stochastic structure implied by the simple search model to interpret the duration data. It is precisely the implication for the dynamics of job acceptance of job-search models which makes them an appealing framework.

(ii) The reservation wage and the duration of unemployment — again

It is now time to shed new light on this key relationship. We have seen that the reservation wage, the probability of leaving unemployment, and the duration of unemployment are intimately linked. In the constant reservation wage model we now know that the (conditional) probability of leaving unemployment in any period is given by equation (5.1) *viz.*:

$$p = [1 - F(r)] \tag{5.1}$$

In a straightforward extension to this, if q is the per period probability of receiving an offer, the probability of leaving unemployment then becomes:

$$p = q[1 - F(r)] \tag{5.2}$$

If reservation wages are not constant then, of course, r requires a time subscript. In general q may be time-dependent also, thus we have:

$$p_t = q_t[1 - F(r_t)] \tag{5.3}$$

Equation (5.3) forms the basis of nearly all the empirical work in this section, and is what Lancaster (1979) calls the *re-employment probability function hazard of failure rate*, or simply the hazard rate. Clearly the probability of not becoming employed in any period is $1 - p_t$. Now let time be a continuous variable so that, to illustrate the necessary notational changes, equation (5.3) is re-written:

$$p(t) = q(t)[1 - F(r(t))] \tag{5.4}$$

which is an 'instantaneous' probability. Within a small period of time from t to $t + dt$, the probability of leaving unemployment is therefore:

$$p(t)dt = q(t)[1 - F(r(t))]dt \tag{5.5}$$

At this stage we introduce a function $G(t)$ which is the distribution function of unemployment durations, or the probability that an individual has an unemployment duration of at most t (weeks). Hence $1 - G(t)$ is the probability of being unemployed for a period in excess of t and may be written in terms of $p(t)$ as;[10]

$$[1 - G(t)] = \exp\left\{-\int_o^t p(x)dx\right\} \tag{5.6}$$

.The expected duration of unemployment for an individual is therefore:

$$\int_o^\infty tg(t)dt = \int_o^\infty [1 - G(t)]\,dt$$

$$= \int_o^\infty \exp\left\{-\int_o^t p(x)dx\right\}dt \tag{5.7}$$

Thus, the stochastic rule (5.6) governing the expected duration of unemployment of an individual depends solely on the sequence of $p(t)$ through time.

Several things emerge from this. First, if evidence of reservation wage behaviour is not available, then there appear to be two ways of proceeding. Either we attempt to estimate reservation wages and observe the behaviour of these estimates over time, in which case we can make inferences about the probability of leaving unemployment using (5.1) (Kiefer and Neumann, 1979a). Alternatively we attempt to estimate $p(t)$s directly and infer the duration properties using (5.6) and (5.7) (Lancaster, 1979; Nickell, 1979; Lancaster and Nickell, 1980). The disadvantage of the former approach is that, by attributing variations in expected duration solely to variations in the reservation wage, the effect of q on duration is ignored unless an independent role is attributed to this variable in the analysis. Thus a study which concludes that reservation wages decline over time (as do most studies) but then infers that the probability of leaving unemployment must therefore be *increasing* are using model (5.1) (with time subscripts) rather than (5.3). The temptation of making the incorrect inference can be seen in Kiefer and Neumann (1979a) who attributed (p. 105) the apparently paradoxical behaviour of $r(t)$ on the one hand and $p(t)$ on the other as 'due to the obvious selectivity biases in the aggregate data' rather than to the neglected variation in $q(t)$. That q should cause such a problem is because as was noted in Barron's (1975) study, a change in q has an ambiguous effect on p. On the one hand, an increase in q increases p directly (through 5.2). On the other hand, since q increases expected returns to search, r is raised thus tending to lower p. Which of these offsetting effects is the strongest cannot be established *a priori*. The ambiguity is easily established formally using the results of exercise 2.3 and equation (5.2).

The disadvantage of the second approach is that since direct estimation of the duration of unemployment (or probability of leaving unemployment) avoids any explicit reference to reservation wage behaviour then studies do not provide direct tests of the alternative job-search hypotheses regarding the behaviour of $r(t)$ over time. In view of the influence of $q(t)$ it is as hard to 'work back' to reservation wage behaviour from evidence on duration as it is to 'work forward' to expected duration from reservation wage behaviour alone. Ideally for this purpose data on reservation wages are required, and some studies (Lancaster and Chesher, 1983; Lynch, 1983) have been built around individual responses to questions about acceptance wages. The approach developed in these papers will be discussed presently.

(iii) The problem of unobservables

In theory, differences between individuals' unemployment experiences or *expected* unemployment duration are due to systematic differences in individual characteristics, only some of which are observable. The central problem then is to capture the effects of unobservable characteristics. One procedure is to assume that an unobservable characteristic (say, 'ability') is distributed across the population in a particular way — for example, acording to a normal distribution — and then to attempt to estimate the parameters of this distribution using sample data. What emerges is then a joint distribution of observables and unobservables. However, this way of accounting for unobservables is sensitive to the choice of functional form chosen for the distribution (Heckman and Singer, 1984a), and the characteristics in question might not be represented in the sample in the same way as they are represented in the population, thus making the resulting inferences of dubious validity. Furthermore, the joint distribution of observables and unobservables may differ between samples, which makes comparison of results obtained from different samples hard to compare (Chesher and Lancaster, 1983).

To illustrate this last point, consider the differences in $p(t)$ between existing unemployed workers (a stock) and those entering unemployment (a flow). Because of 'sorting' (Salant, 1977) — individuals with 'favourable' characteristics, finding jobs sooner and having shorter expected duration — the average duration of unemployment across the sample may be observed to rise even though the expected duration for each individual is constant or even gently falling. This offers an explanation of the apparent paradox — referred to earlier — of observed falling reservation wages *and* falling probabilities of leaving unemployment, and is probably what Kiefer and Neumann (1979a) had in mind when they wrote about 'selectivity biases in the aggregate data'. An implication of this sorting mechanism is that the expected value of $p(t)$ among the existing unemployed will be lower than that among new entrants — the proportion of new entrants likely to find a job in the next week is larger than the proportion of existing unemployed who will do so.

It is natural to ask what it is about individuals which causes them to have different expected durations. What characteristics make some workers more likely to find work than others? This question has occupied a central place in empirical job-search studies for some time, and I turn to the results presently. However, a problem arises when we acknowledge that information on individual characteristics is incomplete, or that not all characteristics are observed. So, for each individual $p(t)$ is going to be determined in part by a set of observable and a set of unobservable characteristics. Now, in principle, differences in the distribution of observables between those already in employment and those entering employment produce systematic and accountable differences in average durations between the two groups if there are no unobservables. However, with unobservables *and* observables having different joint distributions between the stock and flow samples different relationships between average duration and the observables are unaccountable.[11]

In general then, we cannot compare directly the relationship between a vector of observables and, say, $p(t)$ resulting from a study of flows out of unemployment (Kiefer and Neumann, 1979a) with the (different) relationship between the same vector of observables and $p(t)$ resulting from a study of the stock of unemployed (Lancaster, 1979); Nickell, 1979). Although Chesher and Lancaster (1983) have identified some conditions under which valid comparisons may be made they tend to be overly restrictive (that the hazard p should be time-invariant is one of these), and most recent developments are moving away from the reliance on distributional assumptions entirely (Heckman and Singer, 1984a and b). Readers anxious for a detailed econometric survey of the most recent developments are referred to Heckman and Singer (1984c).

As an introduction to this area I consider three approaches. In the first, sample data are used to *estimate* wage offers and reservation wages. In the second set the reservation wage concept is side-stepped and the duration of unemployment (probability of leaving unemployment) estimated directly. In the third, use is made of data on reservation wages.

(iv) Estimation of wage offers and reservation wages
The approach here is developed in two papers by Kiefer and Neumann (1979a and b). The sample is a mixture of those in unemployment (with uncompleted spells) and those who had found work from a group who became unemployed between 1969 and 1973. The survey was taken in 1975. Information was available on the following; education (years), number of dependants, percentage married, percentage union members, percentage local unemployment rate at the time of pay-off, age, unemployment benefit per week (1967 US dollars), maximum duration of benefit, tenure in previous job and previous weekly earnings (in 1967 US dollars). Using the simple constant reservation wage model, the distribution of wage offers for the ith individual with a characteristic vector x_i' is given by:

$$ln\ w_i = x_i'\beta + \epsilon_i \qquad (5.8)$$

where β is a vector of (as yet unknown) parameters and ϵ_i is a normally distributed random variable with zero mean and variance σ_ϵ^2. The reservation wage of individual i is taken to be:

$$ln\, r_i = z_i'\gamma + \mu_i \tag{5.9}$$

where μ_i is a normally distributed random variable with zero mean and variance σ_μ^2, γ a vector of parameters, and z_i' a vector of characteristics. Both ϵ_i and μ_i represent variations in w_i and r_i resulting from unobservables. The joint distribution of ϵ and μ is bivariate normal with covariance $\sigma_{\epsilon\mu}$.

Only accepted wage offers are observed and offers are accepted only if:

$$S_i \equiv ln\, w_i - ln\, r_i > o$$
$$= x_i'\beta - z_i'\gamma + \epsilon_i - \mu_i > o \tag{5.10}$$

The observed wage offer therefore comes from a truncated normal distribution such that (5.10) holds. The truncation implies that the logarithm of observed wage offers has expected value $x_i'\beta + \varrho\sigma_\epsilon\lambda_i$ rather than $x_i'\beta$ as implied by (5.8). Wage offers are therefore determined by the equation:

$$ln\, w_i = x_i'\beta + \varrho\sigma_\epsilon\lambda_i + \epsilon_i - \mu_i \tag{5.11}$$

where $\lambda_i = \phi(-\delta_i)/[1 - \Phi(-\delta_i)]$, $\delta_i = [x_i'\beta - z_i'\gamma]/\sigma$ and $\sigma = (\sigma_\epsilon^2 + \sigma_\mu^2 - 2\sigma_{\epsilon\mu})^{1/2}$. Given information on λ_i allows (5.11) to be estimated giving estimates of β and $\varrho\sigma_\epsilon$. Unfortunately, λ_i itself is something that must be estimated. the overall strategy adopted is to estimate a normalised version of (5.10)[12] by probit (since S_i is a 0 or 1 variable). This generates values of $\hat{\beta}$ and $\hat{\gamma}$ which can be used to generate a series for the λ_i. Equation (5.11) is then estimated using generalised least squares.[13] The probability of finding employment is most strongly affected by the unemployment rate: unemployment benefit does not show up as a significant influence. Wage offers are significantly affected by education, previous job tenure (a negative effect) and the previous wage.

In specifying reservation wage determination, the vector z' contains the whole of the vector x' with some additional search cost variables. However, it is crucial, as in any identification problem, that if we are to be sure that it is reservation wages that we are estimating (and not merely expected wages) then at least some elements of x' must affect reservation wages only via the effect on wages offers and not through any effect they might have on search costs. Otherwise the effects of x' and z' would be indistinguishable. Two variables are therefore assumed not to affect the cost of search, though they have significant effects on the (mean of the) wage-offer distribution; previous job tenure and the previous wage. Variables which are taken to affect search costs but not wage offers are: the number of dependants, marital status, unemployment benefit and maximum duration of these benefits. It is then possible to test whether the identification of these variables with these particular roles is appropriate.

Moving to the results on reservation wages, these are found to be higher the higher are employment benefits and the previous wage.

(v) Duration of unemployment

In three papers, Lancaster and Nickell[14] have avoided the use of the reservation wage concept on the grounds that the behaviour of this variable alone does not give unambiguous predictions of interpersonal or intertemporal variations in the probability of leaving unemployment. The key relationship here is the equation (5.6). Maximum likelihood estimation is used so that the first step is the specification of the likelihood function. The data include both completed and uncompleted spells. Now, the probability that an individual does not find a job in the h periods between selection and interview is $[1 - G(t + h)]/[1 - G(t)]$, while the probability that an individual does find a job at point s ($< h$) is $g(t + s)/[1 - G(t)]$. If n is the number of uncompleted spells and m the number of completed spells, the total likelihood of the sample $n + m$ is:

$$L = \prod_{i=1}^{n} \left[\frac{1 - G_i(t + h)}{1 - G_i(t)} \right] \prod_{j=1}^{m} \left[\frac{g_j(t + s)}{1 - G_j(t)} \right] \qquad (5.12)$$

or since in this case we do not know s but only tht $s < h$, then:

$$L = \prod_{i=1}^{n} \left[\frac{1 - G_i(t + h)}{1 - G_i(t)} \right] \prod_{j=1}^{m} \left[\frac{G_i(t + h) - G_i(t)}{1 - G_j(t)} \right] \qquad (5.13)$$

Secondly, the hazard function must be specified. In general, we know that variations in $p(t)$ are attributable both to variations in $q(t)$ and $F(r(t))$ (equation (5.5)) which depend on individual characteristics and the economic environment. But looked at in this way, we are forced to think explicitly about the reservation wage and its relationship with q. Alternatively, the hazard function can simply be assumed to decompose into two elements, *viz*:

$$p(t) = \psi_1(x)\psi_2(t) \qquad (5.14)$$

in which the effects of individual and market characteristics (the vector x) and the effects of time are given separate consideration. If time plays no role, then $\psi_2(t)$ may be taken as a constant (say, unity), and if $\psi_1(x)$ takes an exponential form then we have;

$$p(t) = \exp\{x'\beta\} \qquad (5.15)$$

Focusing on three variables, age, unemployment rate and the replacement ratio, denoted A, U and B respectively, then

$$ln\,\psi_1 = \beta_o + \beta_1\,ln\,A + \beta_2\,ln\,U + \beta_3\,ln\,B \qquad (5.16)$$

which, gives $p(t)$, $G(t)$ (constants) and hence the likelihood (5.13) directly. The $p(t)$ under this system is time-invariant is unsatisfactory so an alternative form of ψ_2 is specified:[15]

$$\psi_2(t) = \alpha t^{\alpha - 1} \qquad \alpha > o \qquad (5.17)$$

We have already discussed why the behaviour of $p(t)$ over time cannot be established *a priori*, and so (5.17) allows both $\alpha > 1$ (rising $p(t)$) and $\alpha < 1$ (falling $p(t)$), and an estimate of α is obtained when t is included as an independent variable. In this case the expected duration of unemployment is $\exp\{-x'\beta/\alpha\}$.

Empirical results tentatively suggest that $\alpha < 1$ so that $p(t)$ is falling over time. Unfortunately, α is sensitive to the omission of 'heterogeneity' variables. The problem of unobservables appears again. If individuals with a particular characteristic not included in x find jobs sooner than this 'sorting' is picked up as a time effect and not as a characteristic effect, with α 'mopping up' effects which would otherwise be captured by the β coefficient of a *complete* characteristic vector .

To avoid this problem another variable v is introduced into ψ to capture the 'errors' arising from neglected heterogeneity.[16] If v is distributed according to a Gamma distribution with unit mean and variance σ^2 then the distribution function unemployment duration at t given x and v:

$$1 - G(t \mid x, v) = \exp\left\{ - v \exp(x'\beta) \int_o^t \psi_2(u)du \right\} \qquad (5.18)$$

can be transformed into the distribution function of unemployment duration at t given x only by integrating over v, to give:

$$1 - G(t \mid x) = \left[1 + \sigma^2 \exp\{x'\beta\} \int_o^t \psi_2(u)du \right]^{-\sigma^{-2}} \qquad (5.19)$$

with the associated hazard:

$$p_2(t) = \exp\{x'\beta\}\psi_2(t)[1 - G(t \mid x)]^{\sigma^2} \qquad (5.20)$$

which may be called the 'apparent' hazard in which the error has variance σ^2, while the 'true' hazard may be written:

$$p_1(t) = v \exp\{x'\beta\}\psi_2(t) \qquad (5.21)$$

giving the result that if the true hazard is constant, then the apparent hazard is falling. More interestingly, if the true hazard is increasing it is possible for the apparent hazard to be falling.

The model (5.19), allowing for error, is estimated for the case in which $\int_o^t \psi_2(u)du = t^\alpha$. The key results are that the unemployment probability is lower the larger are age, unemployment and the replacement ratio. On the whole though it is not clear whether $\alpha > 1$ or $\alpha < 1$, which leads Lancaster to suggest that duration data are likely to continue to prove unhelpful in isolating the behaviour of the reservation wage.

(vi) Reservation wage data
In the face of the obvious econometric difficulties of controlling for all the various influences on the duration of unemployment, Lancaster and Chesher (1983) have proposed

a way of deducing various effects using the implications of a specific search model and information on reservation wages and expectations of post search remuneration.

The search model used implies that the reservation wage satisfies:

$$r = b + \frac{q}{i} \int_r^\infty [1 - F(w)]\, dw \qquad (5.22)$$

where i is a discount rate, b is the unemployment benefit, q is the probability of receiving an offer in each period $F(.)$ the distribution function of wage offers and r the reservation wage.[17]

The data are derived from the answers to two questions in a UK cross-section study:

(a) How much take home pay would you expect to be able to earn in a new job?
(b) Would you tell me the lowest amount you would be prepared to accept after stoppages?

The answer to (a) is treated as $E[W \mid W \gtrless r]$ rather than $E[W]$, while the answer to (b) is interpreted as r. Using (5.22), the fact that

$$E[W \mid W \gtrless r] = \int_r^\infty W dF(W)/[1 - F(r)]$$

$$= r + \int_r^\infty [1 - F(W)]\, dW/[1 - F(r)] \qquad (5.23)$$

and the hazard function, (5.2), magnitudes can be established for:

$$\frac{\partial lnr}{\partial lnb} = \frac{b}{r} \left[\frac{1}{1 + p/i} \right] \qquad (5.24)$$

$$\frac{\partial lnp}{\partial lnb} = \frac{-f(r)}{[1 - F(r)]} \left[\frac{b}{1 + p/i} \right] \qquad (5.25)$$

$$\frac{\partial lnr}{\partial lnq} = \frac{1}{r} \left[\frac{r - b}{1 + p/i} \right] \qquad (5.25)$$

$$\frac{\partial lnp}{\partial lnq} = 1 - \frac{f(r)}{[1 - F(r)]} \left[\frac{r - b}{1 + p/i}\right] \tag{5.26}$$

But using (5.23) and the hazard function, $p \, dt = q[1 - F(r)]dt$, it appears that $p/i = (r - b)/(x - r)$ where $x = E[W/W \gtrless r]$, giving:

$$\frac{\partial lnr}{\partial lnb} = \frac{b}{r} \left[\frac{x - r}{x - b}\right] \tag{5.24'}$$

$$\frac{\partial lnr}{\partial lnq} = \frac{r - b}{r} \left[\frac{x - r}{x - b}\right] \tag{5.26'}$$

which can be calculated directly using the data on r, x and b. Unfortunately, values for (5.25) and (5.27) require additional assumptions about the form of $F(W)$, or at least the form of the 'hazard' function given in this case by $f(r)/[1 - F(r)]$.

We have seen that the relationship between r and p is rather tenuous, and it would be inappropriate to infer from the reservation wage effects any quantitative predictions about duration. In any case, given the methodology of the approach direct effects of b and q on p can be deduced from (5.25) and (5.27) as long as we are prepared to make assumptions about the hazard rate. Any distribution might suffice for this — though clearly distribution with few parameters are preferred — the Pareto, exponential and normal distributions come to mind.

5.4 EMPIRICAL IMPORTANCE

In the study by Lynch (1983) the amount of wage dispersion facing young unemployed people is somewhat larger than found for other (older) samples ($\sigma = 0.19$) compared with 0.14 in the Kiefer and Neumann (1981) study, and this is identified with the return-to-search concept. Whereas a strict interpretation of the simple search model is that the unemployed are homogeneous and jobs are identical except for the wage on offer, most observed variation in wages disappears when differences between workers and jobs are controlled for. This has led some authors to conclude that the 'pure' gains from search are insignificant and that, as a consequence, search models can explain few market phenomena.

The problem with this view is that it rests on only the simplest of job-search models and on its partial equilibrium properties. As we saw in Chapter 4 (on most acceptable concepts of equilibrium and with well-behaved adjusted processes) market equilibrium, including wage dispersion, requires some form of worker and firm heterogeneity. It is therefore unnecessary to attempt to 'unearth' the pure returns to search by eliminating difference between workers and firms. Heterogeneity is very much a part of search theory and is incorporated quite easily. That most recent empirical work has made use of this fact in an attempt to pin down differences in unemployment duration is encouraging.

Another issue which arises under empirical importance is that of the random search model as a *description* of how workers actually find jobs. The majority of theoretical search models are built around the assumption of random search involving *direct* contact between workers and firms involving no intermediate information-pooling agency. As a description the model is clearly deficient. The evidence is that most workers do not search randomly (Barron and Gilley, 1981) and that more than one search method is employed by most searchers. Referring back to Table 1.1 (p. 6), the importance of intermediate agencies in bringing workers and jobs together is immediately apparent.

The empirical importance of search theories therefore lies not in their descriptive power but in their usefulness in interpreting very strong tendencies in the behaviour of groups of unemployed.

5.5 CONCLUSION

I conclude by summarising some quantitative results on the behaviour of the unemployed.

The *structure* of unemployment puts unemployment statistics in context. It makes a great difference both for policy and for welfare if 3 million unemployed have an average spell of two months or an average spell of twelve months or more on the register. Furthermore, since not all sub-groups of the unemployed can expect to have the same experience, it is important and convenient to identify those who are likely to have particularly long durations.

Approaching these issues via the reservation wage concept is fraught with difficulties (as we have seen), and temptations to make simple inferences about duration from reservation wage evidence must be resisted. The evidence is that reservation wages are modestly time-trended in a downward direction, though apparently less so for the young (Stephenson, 1976, Lynch, 1983), and that this is due to differences in perceived market opportunities and in the arrival rate of offers. This latter effect is responsible for making expected duration only a loose function of the reservation wage.

Without question the most often quoted and most controversial results from empirical studies concern the effect of unemployment benefit on the duration of unemployment. It would be wrong to believe that any consensus exists on the 'disincentive effects', and support may be found for practically any view. The following qualifications should be borne in mind continually when reading the statistics below.

(a) Results have been shown to be sensitive to econometric specification, sample group, definition of replacement ratio (often taken as the ratio of benefit to previous net earnings) and interpretation of reservation wage data.
(b) Large standard errors mean that point estimates are unreliable. In other words, it is misleading to quote single elasticity values without referring to the possible (often quite large) range of variations.
(c) Most studies are based on data from the mid-1970s or earlier. Since the labour market conditions prevailing at that time were quite different from those current in the UK and US, it is unlikely that the predictive or prescriptive power of the results is at all reliable.

(i) UK results
The most often quoted statistic for the UK is based on the work of Lancaster (1979) and Nickell (1979) who find an elasticity of re-employment probability with respect to the

replacement ratio of around -0.6. The data are based on surveys of (predominantly) unemployed males in the early 1970s — the *Political and Economic Planning Unemployment Survey* of 1973 (479 cases) in the Lancaster study, and the *General Household Survey* of 1972 (426 cases) in Nickell's study.

More recently Atkinson *et al.* (1984) have produced a variety of estimates based on different replacement ratio assumptions and using a different sample — 1231 cases of males form the *Family Expenditure Surveys* 1972–77. Estimates of the elasticity vary from -0.12 to less than -1.0 by changes in the replacement ratio, or simply by changing the assumptions about the benefit pattern.

Using the methodology of Lancaster and Chesher (1983), Lynch (1983) has used a survey of 1922 young people in London carried out in 1980. The elasticity re-employemnt probability to unemployment benefit ranged from -0.439 to -0.619 depending on the assumed underlying wage offer distribution, race and sex.

(ii) US results
Feldstein and Poterba (1984) used a sample of 3238 unemployed drawn from the *Current Population Survey*, May 1976. The results show very large, more than proportional, effects of a change in unemployment benefit on re-employment probability. The results, however, are not strictly comparable with the UK evidence; the benefit system differs in important ways and the 'indirect' method is used (making inferences from reservation wage behaviour).

6 Contributions to Microeconomic Theory

6.1 INTRODUCTION

The subject of the first four chapters easily falls under the heading of microeconomics, being concerned with individual behaviour and the implication of this behaviour for the working of markets. However, the concerns of most microeconomics texts are missing from the treatment; consumption and allocation of time decisions, the firm's input choice and price-output decisions, and the efficiency of market equilibrium. In this chapter I set out some relationships between these traditional concerns and search theory.

Job-search decisions do not take place in isolation, and the convenience of assuming that they do is now to be abandoned. A key difference however between the static microeconomic theory and that implied by the search framework is the dynamic nature of the problem prompted by an uncertain environment. Thus the integration of search theory into microeconomics involves inevitably a recasting of the latter to allow for uncertainty and time considerations.

In the following section the dynamics of the individual consumption decision is studied for the case in which the consumer is actively searching for a job or for an improved wage offer; while section 6.3 examines the problem of the allocation of time between search, leisure and work. Of course we know that, in general, the consumption and time-allocation decisions are not independent in a fully specified model of household behaviour, and section 6.3 also discusses some of the interplay between these.

The issue of how work incentives are affected by unemployment insurance and unemployment benefit is treated in some detail in section 6.4. The theoretical consideration are more involved than is suggested by many discussions of the incentive effects of unemployment (as in Chapter 2, for example). Implications of search theory for the theory of the firm are discussed in section 6.5, while problems of allocative efficiency of search markets are studied in section 6.6.

6.2   JOB SEARCH AND CONSUMPTION

The class of problems to be studied in this and the following sections involves an extension, along the time dimension, of the constrained utility-maximisation framework of consumer theory. The individual maximizes utility from consumption and leisure over time rather than the present value of lifetime income. That the focus of attention should be on consumption and the time to enjoy consuming is, in view of neoclassical theory, natural enough, but there is still an important role for income, assets and borrowing via the budget constraint. For the job-searcher, whether currently employed or not, lifetime income is uncertain — hence the problem.

For the most part we assume that per period (instantaneous) utility is given by a smooth function $u(x, l)$ where x is a composite consumption good or consumption bundle and l is leisure time. Somewhat aritificially, in view of the close relationship between choice of x and l, I restrict attention in this section to an examination of choice of x when income — generated by a job search process — is uncertain. Problems including the joint determination of x and l will be discussed in the following section.

The principal studies of the consumption and job-search problem are those of Siven (1974), Seater (1977) and Danforth (1979). In the first two of these the consumption and time-allocation decisions are taken simultaneously and will therefore be discussed in the following section.

The Danforth (1979) model has some interesting features. First, the time-allocation problem is ignored, and transitions occur only between the unemployed to the employed state (and not vice versa). Secondly, lifetime utility depends only on the lifetime consumption pattern in such a way that, for an individual with a (finite) lifetime of T, lifetime utility is given by;

$$U(x(1), \ldots, x(T)) = \sum_{t=1}^{T} \varrho^t u(x(t)) \qquad (6.1)$$

where ϱ is a discount factor and $U(x(t))$ the periodic utility function, which is assumed to exhibit decreasing absolute risk-aversion. The object of choice in each period is consumption $x(t)$, though the constraints on consumer choice depend critically on whether the individual is employed (with certain income) in t or unemployed (with uncertain income). If the individual is engaged in search unemployment prior to date t, consumption at t must be chosen before a wage offer is observed. Assuming that the unit price of $x(t)$ is one, assets at time t are:

$$A(t) = [A(t-1) - x(t-1) - c](1+i) \qquad (6.2)$$

if the individual is unemployed up to the previous period, $t-1$ and;

$$A(t) = [A(t-1) - x(t-1) - w](1+i) \qquad (6.3)$$

if the individual is employed in $t-1$. The per period search cost, wage offer and market interest rate are given by c, w and i, respectively. Further, if the individual is allowed to borrow so long as total debts outstanding at the end of the Tth period do not exceed B, then assets at time t must cover total liabilities, *viz.*:

$$A(t) \geqslant \sum_{1=t}^{T} c(1+i)^{t-1} - \varrho^{N+1-t} B \equiv L_{N-t+1} \qquad (6.4)$$

when the individual is unemployed and;

$$A(t) \geqslant \sum_{1=t}^{T} w(1+i)^{t-T} - \varrho^{N+1-t} B \equiv L_{N-t+1}^w \qquad (6.5)$$

when employed. Total liabilities for the unemployed, L_{N-t+1} are the present value of search costs incurred in each future period less the discounted value of the individual's final period 'credit limit'. Total liabilities for the employed are negative, being the sum of the present values of lifetime income and final period 'credit limit'. The constraint in (6.4) is particularly strict. From current assets it must be possible to finance an entire lifetime of unemployment. Clearly, in view of (6.4) and (6.5), an individual's consumption in period t cannot exceed $A(t) - L_{N-t+1}$ if unemployed or $A(t) - L_{N-t+1}^w$ if employed.

The problem involves the choice of $x(t)$ in each period so as to maximise utility. In the case of an unemployed searcher, a chosen $x(t)$ *implies* a reservation wage as a function of the individual's asset level. Denote by $V_t(A)$ the maximal attainable utility for an individual unemployed at t with assets equal to A and by $U_t(A, w)$ the maximal expected utility attainable for an individual employed at t in a job paying w per year period with assets of A, then, if the reservation wage at t is $r_t(A)$, we have:

$$V_t(A) = \max_x \Big\{ u(x) + \varrho \int^\infty U_{t+1}[(A - x - c)(1 + r), w]\, dF(w)$$

$$r_{t+1}[(A - x - c)(1 + r)]$$

$$+ \varrho V_{t+1}[(A - x - c)(1 + r)] F[r_{t+1}([A - x - c]$$

$$[1 + r])] \Big\} \tag{6.6}$$

where $o \leqslant x \leqslant A(t) - L_{n-t+1}$.

The interpretation of (6.6) should be clear since it has analogues in simple search models.

Danforth (1979) then uses (6.6), and the fact that $u(x)$ displays decreasing absolute risk-aversion, to demonstrate the following propositions:

1. The reservation wage in t is larger the greater are assets at t.
2. The expected duration of search is longer the greater are assets.
3. Increasing the duration of search through increased assets increases the expected post-search earnings.[1]

6.3 LABOUR SUPPLY, CONSUMPTION AND JOB SEARCH

The allocation of time decision of conventional labour economics has been studied in a job-search context most thoroughly by Burdett (1979b), while the joint consideration of consumption plans and job search has been studied, as noted in the previous section, by Siven (1974) and Seater (1977).

The Burdett model takes as the objective the maximisation of utility as a function of income and leisure, these being the key elements of the static theory of labour supply.[2] Each 'period' in this discrete time formulation is divided between the fraction spent searching s, the fraction enjoying leisure l and (if the individual is employed) the fraction spent working h. To give the flavour of the model I outline the problem facing an unemployed individual — Burdett treats both this case and the case of an employed person.

In the unemployed state it must be the case that $s + l = 1$, and while utility is increasing in leisure and income, the latter is uncertain and depends on the amount of time devoted to search. As in previous chapters let q denote the probability of finding an offer in any period, then in Burdett's model:

$$q = q(s) \qquad q'(s) > 0, q''(s) \gtreqless 0$$
$$q(0) = 0 \text{ and } s \in [0, 1] \tag{6.7}$$

and per period utility is written;

$$u(y,l) \qquad u_y > 0,\ u_l > 0,\ u_{yl} < 0$$
$$u_{ll} < 0,\ u_{yy}u_{ll} - (u_{yl})^2 > 0 \tag{6.8}$$

where y is income received in the period:

$$y = \begin{cases} b_t \text{ unemployment benefit if unemployed} \\ w \text{ per period wage if employed} \end{cases} \tag{6.9}$$

The individual receives unemployment benefit only for the first τ periods of unemployment, so that $b_t = b$ for $t \leqslant \tau$, and $b_t = 0$ for $t > \tau$. This appears to correspond well with the benefits system in the UK and the US. Hence we anticipate that an individual's behaviour will be different in the time before τ then in the time after τ.

Denote by $U(w)$ the discounted expected utility from being employed at a rate w and V_t the maximum discounted expected utility from being unemployed at t. Even in the infinite horizon case we use the subscript t because we wish to distinguish between period before τ and periods after τ.

On these assumptions the maximand of the problem is increasing in w (and l) so that a reservation wage policy is optimal, we have:

$$V_t = \max_{l, r} \left\{ u(b_t, l) + \varrho q(1 - l) \int_r^\infty U(W) dF(W) \right.$$

$$\left. + \varrho [1 - q(1 - l)[1 - F(r)]] V_{t+1} \right\} \qquad (6.10)$$

where $l \in [0, 1]$. The reading of (6.10) should now be straightforward in view of the definitions. Performing the maximisation in (6.10) gives for the optimal choice of r and l, respectively:

$$\varrho q(1 - l)f(r_t)[V_{t+1} - U(r_t)] = 0$$

$$u_l - \varrho q' \int_{r_t}^\infty [U(r_t) - V_{t+1}] dF(w) = 0 \qquad (6.11)$$

where the subscript t on the reservation wage reflects the fact that the optimal policy depends on whether the individual is qualified for unemployment benefit in t. That this is so is proved in Proposition 1 of Burdett (1979b) summarised as, *the reservation wage and the chosen leisure time in each period falls if $t \leqslant \tau$ and are both constant after τ.*[3]

The integration of consumption and labour supply decisions was first attained in a job-search context by Siven (1974). In this model job-searchers in the labour market are also engaged in price-reducing search activity in the goods market. Search in the goods market is for price reductions for a homogeneous commodity and that in the labour market for wage improvements in otherwise homogeneous jobs. It is assumed that time devoted to job search is at the expense of working time, therefore involving forgone earnings in the present in anticipation of higher earnings and hence higher consumption in the future. However, given distribution of relative prices and relative wage offers the expected gains from search activity in each sphere can be computed and an optimal allocation of time problem solved. Denote by x, p and w the consumption–price combination and current wage chosen by the individual,[4] who also chooses the proportion of time spent working h, the proportion of time searching the commodity market s_p and the proportion of time spent searching the labour market s_w, $1 - h - s_p - s_w = 0$. The following table shows the impact of changes in current w and p on the endogenous variables;

	x	h	s_w	s_p
w	+	+	−	+
p	−	−	−	+

So that, for example, an increase in the current wage increases consumption, labour supply and goods market search, and reduces job search. These results are derived from a continuous time, infinite horizon model which assumes risk-neutrality.

A more general formulation of the problem is due to Seater (1977).[5] Individuals (instantaneous) utility can be written (using previous notation) as $u = (x(t), l(t))$, where $l(t) = 1 - h(t) - s(t)$.[6] Letting p denote product price the individual's asset position changes over time according to:

$$\dot{A}(t) = iA(t) + w(t)h(t) - x(t)p \qquad (6.12)$$

and if the horizon is T we require $A(T) = 0$. The individual is assumed to be currently receiving wages $w(t)$ and the function $q(s(t))$, relating search time to the rate at which vacancies are forthcoming, is as defined in the model of Burdett (1979b). In this continuous time formulation however the probability of failing to improve on the current wage offer during an interval dt is $F(w(t))^{q(s(t))dt}$, from which Seater shows the expected change in wages resulting from duration and proportion $s(t)$ of time to search when currently employed at the wage $w(t)$ is (in the absence of moving costs) a function:

$$g[w(t), s(t)] = -q[s(t)] \int_{w(t)}^{\bar{w}} lnF(W)dW \qquad (6.13)$$

where $\bar{w}$ is the maximum wage offer available in the market.

The problem is:

$$\max_{x, s,} U = \int_{\tau}^{T} u[x(t), 1 - h(t) - s(t)] dt \qquad (6.14)$$

subject to (6.12), and the fact that the real wage improvement the individual can expect at each point in time is given by g/p. The date τ is the present.

The model produces a complete lifetime profile of consumption and allocation of time decisions. For example, when wages are fairly low the individual specialises in more search to generate higher wages. Secondly, an individual never quits to search; that is, $h > 0$. In early life, the worker responds to increased wages by supplying more hours of work. However, the familiar income effect of increased wages on labour supply *may* eventually dominate in later life so that h falls. The effect of w and s is somewhat clearer. Here there is always a dominating income effect eventually, so that the need to search is less and s falls to zero as the horizon T is approached. Finally, the effect of increasing w is always to make the sum of h and s fall in the latter phase of an individual's life so that the amount of leisure-time eventually increases.

Again we can summarise the response of the system to changes in exogenous variables, in this case real assets, the function q and the real wage.[7]

	$x(t)$	$h(t)$	$s(t)$
A/P	+	−	−
q	+	−	?
w/p	+	?	?

The difficulty with the Seater approach is that although initially the 'job search–wage improvement' modelling is in terms of expectations formed in the presence of wage and job contract uncertainty, no risk elements feed into the optimisation of (6.14) because the function g is taken as representing the actual wage improvement. In other words the maximisation is of utility, which depends on (expected) wages rather than of expected utility, with the expectation taken with respect to wages.

Even so, the Seater model represents the most complete specification of the life-cycle behaviour of consumption, job search and labour supply decisions.[8] Allowing for search as a productive use of time and as an income-generating mechanism clearly adds insight to the life-cycle hypothesis of consumption.

6.4 UNEMPLOYMENT BENEFIT AND INCENTIVES

In section 2.3 we observed that in the simple job-search model an increase in unemployment benefit has an identical effect on the reservation wage and unemployment duration as a reduction in the search cost. The role played by unemployment benefit is examined a little more carefully here.

Three features of the simple search model make it unsuitable as a vehicle for a discussion of the effects of unemployment benefits on job-search behaviour. In the first place, unemployment benefit is paid to *all* unemployed workers regardless of how they became unemployed or how long they have been unemployed. Secondly, the possibility of future involuntary job separations occurring in any accepted job is ignored. Individuals are assumed to have a permanent entitlement to an accepted job. Finally, the unemployment benefit payment is independent of the previous wage. Allowing for earnings-related benefits affects the results significantly.

Recent work has attempted to correct for these important institutional details, with interesting results.

To start, note that in the unemployment benefit systems in the UK and US an individual's entitlement differs depending on whether the individual quits to become unemployed or is laid off.[9] If the former, then the individual may not qualify for benefits or may qualify only for reduced benefit. Also, benefits may cease (or be substantially reduced) after a specified time in unemployment.

Burdett (1979a) has given particular attention to these features. Unemployment benefit payments in t take the following form:

$$b_t = \begin{cases} b > 0 & \text{if } t \lessgtr T \\ 0 & \text{if } t > T \end{cases} \tag{6.15}$$

where T is the duration for unemployment benefit entitlement.

In this case, and with infinite horizon, the following characterises the behaviour of the reservation wage (see

Burdett, 1979a, p. 337):

$$
\left.\begin{array}{ll}
r_{t-1} = r_t & \text{if } t > T \\
r_{t-1} > r_t & \text{if } t \leqslant T
\end{array}\right\} \tag{6.16}
$$

thus indicating a declining reservation wage only for the duration of unemployment benefit entitlement.

Now, introduce the idea that a job is characterised, not simply by its wage offer but also by a per period probability of the worker being laid off λ. Hence a 'contract' is a wage and job security pair (w, λ), both of which are observed prior to job acceptance.[10] The possibility of a lay-off in the future affects the problem in the following way. Since the unemployment benefit is received during any future spell of unemployment following a lay-off, not only does an increase in unemployment benefit increase the returns to current unemployment but also it makes future (risky) employment opportunities more attractive. (This point seems to have been first expressed formally by Mortensen, 1977.) The net effect on the reservation wage[11] is ambiguous if the duration of the entitlement to benefit is finite. In particular Burdett (1979a) shows that if $\lambda > 0$ and $T > 0$, then there is a date $t' \leqslant T$ for which:

$$
\frac{dr_t}{db} > 0 \qquad \text{if } t \leqslant t' < T \tag{6.17}
$$

and

$$
\frac{dr_t}{db} > 0 \qquad \text{if } t' < t < T \tag{6.18}
$$

Hence, the long-term unemployed will reduce their reservation wages, becoming less choosy and *increasing* the probability of leaving unemployment. This is because the relative importance of unemployment benefit as a subsidy to current search falls, while its role in augmenting future returns to employment increases. In the absence of any limit on entitlement, we have:

$$
\frac{dr_t}{db} > 0 \qquad \text{all } t \tag{6.17}
$$

the familiar *disincentive* effect.

Interestingly in these models, if the return to search is constant, meaning either that benefit is not earnings-related or that future returns are not influenced by a worker's lay-off history,[12] then the reservation wage r is independent of the lay-off probability λ, (Burdett and Mortensen, 1980), regardless of the worker's attitude to risk (Hey and Mavromaras, 1981).

This result arises because since the reservation wage makes a worker indifferent between searching and working at the reservation wage, an individual accepting only wages above r can ignore the associated λ-value. After all, the worst that can happen is that the individual becomes unemployed again immediately ($\lambda = 1$)!

The reservation wage, however, is not independent of the lay-off probability in general if future returns to search following a lay-off differ from the current returns to search. This will be the case, for example, if benefits are earnings related,[13] although the precise form of the relationship depends on the magnitude of the previous wage relative to the reservation wage (Hey and Mavromaras, 1981).[14]

Returning to incentive effects. It is clearly the structure of the entitlement of unemployment benefit which determines the direction and extent of any incentive effects. Shavell and Weiss (1979) have examined the optimal structure of benefits payments over time. In the case of individuals with no wealth, who cannot borrow and who are risk-averse, a limited total budget should be allocated in such a way that payments decline monotonically with the duration of unemployment. Taking administrative costs into account, the downward (stepped) path of most benefit systems appears to approximate this.[15]

6.5   IMPLICATIONS FOR THE THEORY OF THE FIRM

It is clear from the discussion of Chapter 4 that the firm's role in a search market context has not received great attention. Here, I consider some implications of search theory to be borne in mind when thinking about the firm's role.

(i) Market power and objectives

In a decentralised market firms will have a degree of monopsony power (Arrow, 1959) so that the perfect competition model is inappropriate if we are to understand about employment, turnover and unemployment decisions.

Whatever the firm's objectives it may face a large number of potential choice instruments: its wage structure (which may in part depend on bargaining arrangements); a minimum productivity requirement (which may be partly determined by technology); and its employment level (which may be conditioned by the state of demand). In practice, firms may be constrained to greater or lesser degree in their choice of instruments but in theory, abstracting from *ad hoc* institutional arrangements, the choice set is very rich. From the search theorist's viewpoint this is a great problem.

Without exception, the literature on this topic takes firms as pursuing (short-run) profit-maximisation, and it is as well for us to bear this in mind too since it imposes a certain discipline, eliminating many alternatives which can always be argued on 'managerial discretion' grounds.

In Chapter 4 we saw how a firm may fill a *given* vacancy either by choosing a wage or, if it is constrained in this direction, by choosing the 'right' worker for its needs. Furthermore, in principle, a firm might combine the two, by choosing an *initial* wage and subsequently 'weeding out' unsatisfactory workers.

However, in the traditional theory of the firm the input decision revolves around the number of workers employed and (most often) the single wages paid. The marginal productivity theory for labour demand is at the heart of this. In a dynamic theory of the firm and one with heterogeneous workers, it is hard to see any role for the marginal productivity theory. Furthermore, with turnover and demand changes the firm's employment policy is not a once-for-all decision, but is one of continual adjustment.

(ii) Production

In traditional theory, the marginal product is the result of the technical relationship between the (chosen) size of the labour input and the (fixed in the short run) capital stock. Thus, even workers who are identical *ex ante* have different productivities on combination. Anonymity ensures that who becomes the 'marginal worker' depends on the luck of the draw. A theory of the firm in a search market might be expected to capture this. Certainly, in establishing the firm's choice of employment level when workers are homogeneous, some assumption regarding the internal technology would seem to be essential.

However, in a market of heterogeneous workers the most important source of productivity need not be this technical relationship as such, but rather the ability, effort and attitude of the worker. In fact, it is this which justifies the association of productivity with the *worker* in the model of section 4.4(ii). The disadvantage of this approach, and with any approach which regards productivity as being observable at *some* cost, is that not all sources of variation in productivity are worker-specific. To avoid this (and other complications) some models, especially those dealing with market equilibrium, attribute productivity simply as the result of the quality of the job-match (see Jovanovic, 1984; Pissarides, 1984, for recent examples). In this world the intimacy between marginal productivity and firm size found in the static model is lost. Furthermore, we know that if the quality of the job match is unsatisfactory to at least one side of the bargain, there will be some turnover and the firm's employment level will oscillate. Thus, any interesting equilibria we might look for in search markets are bound to involve some turnover (Diamond, 1982a; Pissarides, 1984, p. 98).

(iii) Lay-offs

An area of analysis of the labour market under uncertainty which developed independently of job-search theory is the *implicit contract* and *temporary lay-off* class of problem. Recent research has shown that these labour market aspects are not inconsistent with search behaviour, and it is in this context that I discuss the work here.

In brief, the work on implicit contracts has established conditions under which contracts between workers and firms involve the use of mutually-agreed periods of temporary lay-off for some workers. Thus, when demand drops temporarily firms lay off workers who are recalled again when demand picks up. The problem for the search theorist is to explain if workers would ever search out alternative employment during a period of lay-off. After all, if a worker has agreed to this type of contract it clearly falls within an acceptance set, so why should alternative contracts be sought? Actually the problem is very similar to that of on-the-job search, though here search is initiated if the probability of recall into the previous employment is low (Pissarides, 1982), or zero (that is, a permanent lay-off) (Cothren, 1983). This recall probability is determined by the depth of the demand depression, and Pissarides (1982) has shown how the job-search problem is affected by the presence of lay-off *and* recall probabilities. However, since these studies take the lay-off probability as given and not derived from an optimising framework, a full integration of search and implicit contract theory has yet to be accomplished.

6.6   JOB SEARCH AND EFFICIENCY

Questions of economic efficiency arise wherever there is a potential conflict between the outcome of individual decision-making and the outcome which would be regarded as most desirable by individuals as a collective — the socially desired outcome.

Of necessity, these questions are discussed in terms of the overall equilibrium outcome; what we referred to in Chapter 4 as the market equilibrium solution. Furthermore, in so far as we can identify an economy-wide equilibrium, then efficiency considerations may be a guide for macroeconomic policy. These issues are discussed in Chapter 7.

For now, I simply want to outline the issues involved in search efficiency. In doing so I shall raise many questions and provide few answers, because this aspect has only recently attracted formal attention, and work is still very much in the early stages of development. Hence, rather then present the details of a specific model, I shall discuss the issues in a quite general way. Many of the themes can be followed up in the quite small literature on this topic.[16]

Of necessity, the models of search equilibrium used to study efficiency questions take very simple forms. The market models of section 4.5 used to study equilibrium wage dispersion are too complex for current purposes. Rather, we stand back and simply look at the search mechanisms as a matching process bringing together vacancies and unemployed workers, and assume that the wage as a *function* of realised profit is the outcome of a bargaining process. The number of matches made will depend on both the number of contacts made (the search technology) and the probability that each 'contact' is successful (that is, leads to a match). In turn, the search technology will depend on the number of vacancies and the number of unemployed workers, while the probability that a job match is made depends on the policy of workers (reservation wages) and firms (reservation profits).

Now, inefficiencies arise in these models because of externalities in the search process. A full discussion of this needs a theory of wage determination, but it is not hard to see how externalities arise. For example, the decision by a firm to open up a vacancy at a particular wage constitutes a *marginal* decision for the firm; that is, the firm is indifferent between opening up the vacancy and not. However, in a *market* context a new vacancy for a given stock of unemployed has two effects. First, it *lowers* the matching opportunities for existing vacancies v, by the additional competition. Secondly, it *raises* the matching opportunities for the unemployed u. The overall effect this has on equilibrium depends principally on whether $v > u$, $v = u$ or $u > v$ (influencing search technology) and on wage determination (influencing job-acceptance policies of both firms and workers). It is clear, however, that if firms create vacancies without regard to the impact on existing market participants, the 'wrong' number of vacancies will be created from society's point of view. Similar remarks apply for worker's job acceptances, where again the effect on the market of a successful match (the losing of an unemployed worker and a vancancy) depends on (among other things) the relative values of v and u.

In a study by Pissarides (1984), for example, the equilibrium amount of unemployment depends on the equilibrium wage rate, but an unambiguous result arises for the amount of turnover in equilibrium. In particular the externalities lead to the setting of reservation wages (and reservation profits) which may be too low from society's viewpoint, so that too few jobs are rejected.

The wage determination discussed in, for example, Diamond (1982) may take a variety of forms, but it essentially involves the division of the surplus resulting from search activity. This surplus arises from the fact that marginal decisions involve the comparison of returns (continued) in the absence of a match with those (expected to) result from a match. In the case of a worker, the decision is marginal if the return to continued search V equals the return to employment, say $U(w)$, which is the condition defining the reservation wage. An equivalent marginal condition for the firm is that the expected value of a vacancy must equal the expected value from filling the vacancy, say W. *In general*, it will be the case that for a successful match $U - V > 0$ (implied by $w > r$) and $W - \pi > 0$. A wage rule in equilibrium therefore determines the share of the joint surplus $U - V + W - \pi$ between firms and workers.

We can imagine other types of externality affecting the market outcome. This involves the search process as a source of information. If information obtained by a searcher can be observed by other 'neighbours' then an external economy has passed between the cost-bearing searcher and the local 'free-riders'. The possibilities here are numerous. For one, with some (limited) information freely available after a 'discovery' the search environment could become unstable, with incentives to undertake costly search activity seriously undermined. However, even with a stable group of willing and active searchers, the information externality may imply that, from society's point of view, too little search is undertaken.

6.7   CONCLUSION

The search theory complements many results of static microeconomic theory. However, two areas are in need of further development. First, the implications of job-search activity for the (dynamic) theory of the firm have yet to be worked out. The models of Chapter 4 take us only a short way in this direction. The analysis of firm size, vacancy creation and the wage–product relation has yet to be formalised.

Secondly, the efficiency of search market equilibrium is a question only recently addressed using simple models. In particular we need to know the efficiency aspects of the break-up of job matches, whereas at present only match-formation is allowed for as an endogenously-determined state transition. Efficiency questions arising from wage dispersion in equilibrium have yet to be addressed.

7 Contributions to Macroeconomic Theory

7.1 INTRODUCTION

The earlier discussion of market equilibrium (section 4.5) and efficiency of search equilibrium (section 6.6) have already taken us close to a macroscopic view of job-search processes. In detail these models are very complex and a useful study of various macroeconomic phenomena is practicable only if the discussion is broadened. This we do now.

The following section discusses the relationship between inflation and unemployment along with the related themes of the 'voluntary' nature of search unemployment, and the unemployment–vacancy relationship. This provides a basis for the discussion of the role of aggregate demand management as a search economy in section 7.3. Some other issues of current macroeconomics are examined in section 7.4. These include the relationship between unemployment benefit and unemployment, and of the role of incomes policies in controlling the economy.

7.2 UNEMPLOYMENT AND INFLATION

The relationship between the rate of change of prices (or wages) and the rate of unemployment has for many years been at the centre of discussion in macroeconomics, and since the early 1970s search theory has been intimately linked with this Phillips curve idea. This association can arise in a number of ways, but the following story appears to be the simplest.

Consider an economy with a stable environment and a pool of unemployed searchers with firmly held (and initially correct) views about the distribution of wage offers, and all using a reservation wage rule. Now let government expenditure increase unexpectedly. Firms attempt to meet demand by increasing output which, for our purposes, can be achieved only by hiring more labour. Now, we know (from Chapter 4) that in search markets firms are able to control the supply of labour by varying the wage rate, so that all firms will attempt to attract more labour by increasing wages. Of course, this general increase in wages improves the wage-offer distribution which, at least in the short run, may not be perceived by the unemployed who continue to search with unchanged reservation wages. The result is that workers now find acceptable jobs more easily than before and unemployment falls, with the extent of the increase in employment determined by the extent of the change in wages. This process decribes a movement along a (short-run) Phillips curve. However, searchers' experience in finding jobs more quickly may lead to a revision of beliefs about the true wage-offer distribution along lines suggested in section 3.7, so that reservation wages will be revised upwards thus tending to reduce the number of workers finding work in any period. In the long run of correctly perceived earnings opportunities the labour market returns to an *equilibrium* level of unemployment.

This sequence of events is often described as *the* job search interpretation of the Phillips curve and as *the* only macroeconomic adjustment process consistent with job-search theory. In fact, neither of these is correct so that the relationship between job-search models and the Phillips curve concept, in both its short-run and long-run manifestations, is a good deal more tenuous than is commonly believed. The relationship is therefore worth closer scrutiny.

The theme of this section is that, even viewed strictly through models of search market behaviour, a variety of macroeconomic adjustment paths are possible, including the one already described and its more sophisticated variants. To develop this theme I suggest a phasing of the process already described as follows:

   (i) firm's behaviour in the face of demand changes,
  (ii) workers' perceptions, opportunities and constraints,
 (iii) short-run adjustments,
 (iv) long-run adjustments.

Each phase will be considered separately, but first I shall present a more detailed analysis of the simple job-search interpretation of macroeconomic adjustment following a sudden increase in demand.[1]

Assume that a market composed of large numbers of firms and workers is in an equilibrium with the following features: vacancies exist and have associated wage offers chosen by the firm; unemployed searchers set reservation wages; there exists a stationary distribution of wage offers across firms and a stationary distribution of reservation wage offers across workers. Suppose now that the government increases its demand for goods. Because supply of output is less than perfectly elastic two changes result in the short run. First, prices rise in aggregate under most assumptions about the degree of competitiveness of the commodity market. Secondly, firms, prompted by new profit opportunities and with a degree of monopsony power created by costs of information, attempt to increase output (by increasing employment) and hence raise money wages. The net effect of increases in prices and money wages on *real* wages is unclear at this stage, because individual firms cannot always ensure that the increase in money wages constitutes a *real* improvement in workers' remunerations. Suppose then, that the distribution of wages expressed in real terms[2] shifts to the right.

At this point the behaviour of workers is crucial. In a stable environment the perceived distribution of wage offers may well coincide with the actual. However, following a (possibly unexpected) stimulus, a shift in the wage-offer distribution may go undetected or may be underestimated, in which case reservation wages will fall *relative* to the new distribution, leading to an increase in the numbers finding work in each period. Moreover, the number of additional searchers finding jobs will depend on the *extent* of the shift in the distribution of wage offers. The larger are the wage increases the greater is the fall in search unemployment, because the distribution of wage offers shifts relative to the *distribution* of reservation wages.

To illustrate, consider firm i and its wage adjustment from w_i to $w_i'(w_i < w_i')$ then clearly, given a distribution of reservation wages, more workers will find w_i' attractive the greater is $w_i' - w_i$. Thus an 8 per cent one-period wage inflation may lead to a drop in the unemployment rate from 12 to 8 per cent while a 15 per cent inflation would lead to a fall in unemployment to 6 per cent. This case is illustrated in Figure 7.1.

If, in the following period, searchers realise that the distribution has changed then they will revise reservation wages upwards and unemployment will increase, as previously acceptable jobs become unacceptable. Firms can only keep ahead by raising wages still further and can only maintain high employment by persistently inflating wage offers. In terms of the example of Figure 7.1, as workers realise their mistake in not raising reservation wages the unemployment rate will return to 12 per cent while the point A — a disequilibrium as far as workers are concerned — can be maintained by a period-on-period inflation of 8 per cent as reservation wages increase (by 8 per cent) with, say, a one period lag.

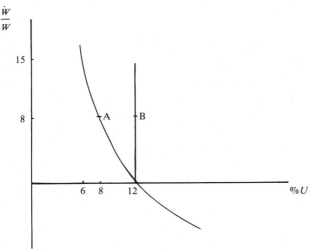

Figure 7.1: Short-run Phillips curve

Notice that whether point A can be maintained depends in this search explanation on reservation wage adjustment lagging behind changes in the wage-offer distribution. If workers come to anticipate (correctly) the continued 8 per cent inflation, then reservation wages will change period-by-period to reflect this, and a correctly perceived inflation will have no effect on unemployment so that only point B is attainable. Since, it is often argued, expectations will be correct in the long run, point B constitutes an equilibrium for the economy. This brings about the conclusion, often associated with Friedman (1968) and Phelps (1967), of the long-run ineffectiveness of policy activism.

(i)   Firms' behaviour in the face of demand changes[3]

As was noted by Pissarides (1976a) and in our Chapter 4, dynamics of search markets do not rely entirely on the firm making wage adjustments. With continual labour turnover, costs of wage adjustment[4] and heterogeneous workers, other responses to a demand increase are possible. For example, the firm may adjust its internal policies to reduce turn-over by improving job conditions (reducing quits) and by relaxing its recruitment policy (reducing dismissals).

In terms of the discussion of Chapter 4, it is clear that the Phillips curve dynamics result from a 'flexwage' environment, whereas a 'fixwage' adjustment path may have no immediate inflationary implications. For example, a 'fixwage' adjustment path in face of a demand increase appears to imply a reduction in turnover, a lower marginal product (since a lowering of the recruitment standard makes the firm's 'marginal worker' likely to be less productive than previously), and increased employment. However, by becoming less choosy, firms may improve market opportunities for workers and reservation wages may be increased in view of the new job prospects. Even if the wage offer distribution remains unchanged, the distribution of reservation wages may *increase* relative to the wage offer distribution — a result contrary to the short-run 'flexwage' dynamic. The result is that a reduction in job separation may be accompanied by a corresponding reduction in the take-up of jobs, and how

these offsetting forces affect unemployment is hard to say *a priori*.
. Under this system, though, there appears to be some scope for output gains with little inflation. If a 'fixwage' path increases employment an expansion of demand may be self-financing. In other words, in a 'fixwage' economy the aggregate supply curve will be more elastic than in the 'flexwage' case — a proposition which is essentially a restatement of the multiplier process (Pissarides, 1976a, pp. 229 *et seq.*). Unfortunately, search theory at present is unable to offer a convincing theory of how expansions of nominal demand are apportioned between output changes and price changes. In other words, search theory alone does not make endogenous the 'fixwage'–'flexwage' distinction.

Many firms are so constrained that neither wage adjustments nor quantity adjustments are possible. This leaves the intensive margin to operate on, and we know that firms change the utilisation of the existing workforce quite markedly over the cycle. The reasons for this are quite clear. When there are both barriers to wage adjustment and fixed employment costs the firm finds it easier to reach agreement on changes in work practices with its existing workforce. The use of overtime during demand expansions and part-time or temporary lay-offs during demand contractions are common practices. On the whole, however, these adjustments are regarded as short-run, stop-gap measures designed to see the firm through uncertain times and their impact on a job-search interpretation of macroeconomic adjustments are relatively minor. However, temporary lay-offs and search theory do have some points of common contact, and I discuss these in the section 7.3.

(ii)   Workers' perceptions, opportunities and constraints
Several issues arise from the behaviour of workers posited by the simple search interpretation of the Phillips curve.

One source of irritation is that in describing the initial stationary state the simple search model of Chapter 2 is assumed. However, the short-run dynamics are impossible without misperceptions of the wage-offer distribution. Not only is this very crude theorising, but it may give a totally

misleading interpretation of events. The problem here is that
of a searcher's behaviour when the distribution is unknown
and wage offers contain information about the wage-offer
distribution as well as a potential source of earnings. We
know that in ⁺his case a reservation wage need not be unique,
implying that leftward shifts in the distribution need not
necessarily bring forth any additional labour. Of course, in
the aggregate these theoretical issues may not matter, but it
is worth noting that if firms are unsure about the effectiveness of wage increase in bringing forth more labour they
may be less likely to take a chance with a 'flexwage' policy.

More important is the presumption that the shift in the
wage-offer distribution has an unambiguous effect on the
level of unemployment. This, as I hope to show, relies on a
quite static view of both the pool of unemployed searchers
and the stock of employed workers.

Ignoring for the moment those moving from employment
into unemployment, *two* flows have a significant impact on
the stock of unemployed: those finding employment and
those who move from non-participation into participation.
Both of these flows are affected by an improvement in the
wage-offer distribution, and the argument that unemployment will at first fall and then rise back to its initial level
(Figure 7.1) takes the participation rate as given. There are,
on the contrary, several possibilities. For example, the
unemployment which emerges as workers realise that the
distribution of wages has improved may be reinforced by the
increase in registered unemployment by new participants
attracted by the higher returns to search. The precise
dynamic path will depend on, *inter alia*, the speed with which
non-participants discover the higher returns to search and the
behaviour of existing participants. This 'added worker'
effect may trace out a *positively* sloped Phillips curve and, in
terms of Figure 7.1, instead of returning to point B, the
economy's registered unemployment level may increase
beyond B. Exactly where the unemployment rate will settle is
not certain, especially if some of the new participants, realis-
ing the increased competition from existing participants, are
'discouraged' into non-participation once more. Whatever
the precise adjustment path, there is no compelling reason to

expect a stable short-run unemployment vacancy relationship in a search market. These issues are discussed more formally in McCafferty (1980).

The general improvement in wage offers, once realised, is not simply an added benefit for the unemployed. In general, the unemployed are in competition for jobs with those already employed who are seeking wage improvements. Indeed, on-the-job searchers may have better information about opportunities and, by virtue of being employed, may make a more favourable impression on prospective employers. If we imagine an implicit 'pecking order' by which wage-improvers find the better jobs, the unemployed (having revised upwards their expectations and reservation wages) may be left with the relatively low-paid jobs which, at least for a time, they will reject. The actual prospects facing the unemployed in this case may not warrant upward revision of reservation wages. As workers realise *this* error and lower their reservation wages unemployment will drop.

These two examples, taking account of the effect on participation and on existing workers of a general wage improvement, produce rather different dynamic paths than does the simple explanation.

The mechanism by which unemployment increases as workers raise their reservation wages is also worth closer scrutiny. New participants apart, the argument here is that those who have accepted jobs using the 'wrong' reservation wage will increase their reservation wages and quit to seek out new opportunities. There appear to be two difficulties with this. First, individuals — even those who realise they have made a mistake — rarely quit in favour of unemployment. Secondly, as we saw in Chapter 3, the circumstances faced by, and hence the decision criteria used by, on-the-job searchers are quite different from those of the unemployed. Given moving costs, the required reservation wage revision to induce a quit may be substantial and it is unlikely that all of those who (incorrectly) accepted jobs will return to unemployment. There is bound to be some net absorption into employment, and the economy is unlikely to be carried back to its initial unemployment rate unless participation increases by just the right amount. It appears that although searchers cannot be 'fooled' indefinitely, the effects of workers having misperceived the distribution are not totally reversible.

So far I have assumed that the increase in money wages by firms constitutes a *real* wage improvement for workers, and the dynamics outlined have been generated by the delays in perceiving real wage changes. The question of whether real wage improvements themselves can be sustained is an important issue in macroeconomics and I turn to this and other broader issues now.

(iii) Short-run adjustments
In many modern treatments, the explanation of movements such as that from A to B in Figure 7.1 relies on a divergence of actual real wage changes by employers from those perceived by workers. This divergence, often explained in terms of 'money illusion' or faulty price expectations, initially causes the movement of the short-run Phillips curve to point A. Subsequently correction of faulty price expectations moves the economy from A to B. In very broad terms, the dynamics resulting from faulty price expectations are similar to those resulting from misperceptions of the wage offer distribution.

In this section I consider the more traditional explanation of the short-run dynamics — involving price expectations — and show how these considerations fit in with a job-search interpretation. The aim is to build an overall picture of short-run dynamics.

Suppose once more that in response to a sudden increase in demand firms raise money wages in an attempt to attract more labour but this time, for simplicity, the wage increases are fully perceived by job-searchers. Two questions now arise. What happens to prices? How do workers *perceive* price movements?[5] Suppose for simplicity that money wages and prices move proportionately to leave the actual real wage unchanged, then employment fluctuations can arise only if workers form incorrect expectations about price movements. If workers underestimate the increase in prices they will *perceive* an increase in the real wage and supply more labour taking unemployment below its equilibrium level, while an overestimate or anticipation of a price increase will take employment above its equilibrium level. Once price expectations are correct unemployment returns to the equilibrium level.[6] In the short run the path generated by faulty perceptions traces the Phillips curve relation of Figure 7.1; or alternatively the Lucas aggregate supply curve, in which output increases (unemployment falls) as long as price expectations lag behind actual price movements.

At this point we might enquire into why actual prices move proportionately with money wages to leave real wages unchanged. This is not the place to delve deeply into this issue, but such equiproportioned movements in money wages and prices are a strong result derived from a theory of the neutrality of nominal variables (Friedman, 1968). On the other hand, various institutional (Okun, 1981) and choice-theoretic arguments using costs of adjustment arguments may be used to weaken the neutrality results. Whatever one's view on this, the issue of how expectations are formed is quite distinct.

Whilst recognising the existence of others, I shall consider two price expectations mechanisms, both of which figure prominently in the macroeconomic literature. Under *adaptive expectations*, forecasts of price movements depend solely on previous price movements. In stable environments and when price movements are not trended, this represents a relatively simple and intuitively appealing concept. However, given that price movements often oscillate around a trend, agents may do better by anticipating price movements based on information about both policy changes and the relationship between policy parameters and prices. In other words, information about future price movements is available from a large number of sources, and a *rational* expectation uses the available information in the best possible way.

The implication of this is that while under adaptive expectations forecast prices may lag behind actual prices (where the latter are increasing) for quite long periods, under rational expectations only genuine surprises will cause a deviation between actual and perceived prices.

A more complete picture of short-run dynamics is now possible. For a given demand stimulus we shall trace out paths for the following macroeconomic variables: unemployment, employment, consumption and inflation. For simplicity, I shall assume that *on average* actual prices and money wages vary proportionately. Attention then focuses on the *perceived* change in real wages.

In view of our discussion we can identify two sources of the misperception of real wages: the extent of the change in money wages and the change of the cost in living. I shall assume that the latter affects all workers equally, in the sense that all individuals use the same price deflator in their real income calculations. In the case of changes in money wages, the shift in the distribution which retains the proportionality between average wages and prices *may* be in the form of equal increases in *all* money wages. In this case the distribution shifts uniformly to the right. However, constant average real wages may result from endless other changes as different firms make different wage adjustments. There may be many reasons for this. First, the increase in demand will not be shared out equally among firms, which will lead to different product price and wage adjustments. Secondly, even if the demand stimulus is evenly distributed, firms in different market environments will respond differently. Finally, although workers, in calculating *their* real wage changes, will construct a price index based on their consumption bundles, firms will base their real wage calculation on own-product price. There is therefore wide scope for the extent of money wage revision to differ between firms.

Suppose that all firms do make the same money wage adjustment so that the actual money wage distribution shifts uniformly to the right. Further, suppose that workers form rational expectations about the effect of the government policy on wages and prices. The result, in this case is that no workers will adjust their reservation wages — even in the short run — and there will be no movement away from equilibrium employment. Under adaptive expectations the adjustment path depends on whether workers perceive changes in the price level before perceiving changes in the money wage offer distribution. It may be that the continuous act of consumption makes searchers more aware of price changes, making the distribution of *real* wages appear to have shifted to the left uniformly. The distribution of reservation wages will therefore shift to the left relative to the actual (unchanged) distribution of real wages and searchers will be absorbed into employment more quickly. On the other hand, if it is the increase in money wages which workers perceive first reservation wages will rise causing more prolonged periods of search, suggesting a positively-sloped short-run Phillips curve. In both cases, as misperceptions are corrected, the economy returns to the equilibrium employment level.

If all firms do not make the same wage adjustment the dynamics are more complex, and since the possible adjustment paths are large in number, I shall confine myself here to some general remarks.

The crucial point is that even if agents form rational expectations about the *average* real wage, unless the distribution of real wages retains its *shape* after money-wage adjustments, workers will not be indifferent between the distributions in general. As we saw in Chapter 2, even risk-neutral workers have reservation wages which are sensitive to changes in wage dispersion. The final configuration of distribution of wages and reservation wages is unclear, but an unchanged average real wage is not necessarily bound with an unchanged employment level in this case, since *optimal* adjustments in reservation wages relative to the wage offer distribution may be permanent.

(iv) Long-run adjustments

The concept of the long run in explanations of the Phillips curve phenomenon tends to depend on the full realisation of mistakes and the correction of misperceptions. Therefore, in the long run the economy is in equilibrium in the sense that decisions are based on correct information.[7] In other areas of economics the long run is associated with full structural adjustment of the economy through changes in the capital stock, technical innovation and market institutions. Because of all these long-run influences, the equilibrium employment resulting from fully perceived opportunities must be regarded as a function and not as a particular level.

Hence the idea that increases in aggregate demand have no

long-run consequences for output amounts to the notion that increases in demand have no supply-side consequences. I turn to these issues presently.

Before examining the role of aggregate demand in a search economy I turn to an issue which generates much heated discussion. The question often arises as to whether workers who behave in the way discussed in the job-search literature are *voluntarily* unemployed.

First, there is nothing in the mechanics of search theory which makes a spell of unemployment entirely voluntary. Success in leaving unemployment depends on three things: discovering a job, being suitable for a job, and finding a job acceptable. Only the last of these is entirely at the searcher's discretion. Failure in the first two may force an otherwise willing worker to remain unemployed — perhaps for a considerable length of time. In view of the great costs involved it is not always obvious to an unemployed searcher that a change of location or skill is either necessary or feasible.

The view that unemployment is voluntary is often accompanied by the view that society would be better-off (in terms of lower unemployment) if individuals were forced into the position of accepting jobs they might normally reject. This is not an implication derived from job-search theory. On the contrary, there are good theoretical reasons for believing that the amount of job rejection by searchers is too low. In addition to the argument offered by Pissarides (1984) based on externalities (see section 6.6), in a world of heterogeneous firms and workers society would not be indifferent to a worker with one set of skills accepting employment in a job requiring other skills if only lack of information prevents a more suitable applicant from filling the vacancy. Given training costs and the extra turnover likely from workers and firms being dissatisfied with poor matches, society might prefer the vacancy to remain open longer. Society's preferences may not be reflected in individual decisions because the private consequences of a particular match do not reflect society's losses until the true value of the match is realised. At the time matches are made, both workers and firms may have an over-optimistic view of the expected pay-off.

Thus, even if unemployment is 'voluntary', a policy which

increases job acceptances may result in matches which society would be better-off without.

7.3   AGGREGATE DEMAND

In view of the preceding discussion there appear to be good grounds for doubting any particular relationship between aggregate demand changes and unemployment. Even so, the idea that the level of unemployment cannot be affected in the long run by demand changes is shared by many macroeconomists. The argument of this section is that this strong result is not supported by a theory which allows for uncertainties in job matching.

In an early critique Grossman (1973) suggested that, as a theory relating aggregate demand to unemployment, search theory is deficient in three respects. First, that the theory makes no allowance for involuntary separation and job shortages; secondly, that (short-run) cyclical movements in employment are accompanied by countercyclical movements in real wages; this leads to the third deficiency, that increases in employment are accompanied by *reduced* consumption expenditures. None of these, argues Grossman, is justified on empirical grounds. It should now be clear that these criticisms are aimed at a very naïve job-search theory, and that the short-run dynamics derived from more general models are able to meet many of Grossman's points.

However, Grossman is primarily concerned with cyclical behaviour, while much of the attention in recent times has been on the relationship between aggregate demand and the (long-run) equilibrium unemployment rate. The challenge to the theory underlying economic policy in both the UK and the US since 1945 is the argument, often based on static market clearing models, that aggregate demand exerts no durable influences on the level of real economic activity.

On the contrary, however, recent research on the effects of aggregate demand on search unemployment indicates that equilibrium unemployment (in the sense used in this chapter) is not in general independent of the level of aggregate demand. There was a hint of this earlier in the description of the consequences following from differential wage adjustments by firms. In this case, the impact of aggregate demand on employment is ambiguous because whether an individual perceives a change in the distribution as favourable depends on the searcher's reservation wage relative to the wage-offer distribution, and on which part of the distribution is experiencing the greatest wage increases.[8] Unfortunately, the full implications of any initial change in the distribution of real wages requires a general equilibrium model of a degree of sophistication that is unavailable to us at present. Not only will workers respond to changes in the real wage offer distribution by establishing a new distribution of reservation wages, but this in turn, by affecting labour supply to each firm, will prompt a wage-setting reaction.

Recently, Diamond (1982b) has addressed the issue of aggregate demand influences in a much simpler search framework, though some of his general conclusions are clearly appropriate for more elaborate models.

In search equilibrium (except in the trivial case of no unemployment and no vacancies) there are unrealised employment oportunities due to information costs, and since externalities then prevent the 'right' amount of search taking place, the government can use resources to bring agents together. Most obviously, for example, an increase in government expenditure, by creating new vacancies can increase the probability of a successful job match, and there is nothing in the job-search theory to say that, as a result, reservation wages will be revised upwards to the extent that the (average) probability of leaving unemployment will remain unchanged. However, there is no presumption in Diamond's analysis that all reductions in unemployment by demand expansion are desirable, even if they are possible. The point is simply that increased demand may potentially improve the matching process, reduce friction and lower the equilibrium rate of unemployment. In this world 'natural rate' of unemployment is not unique, and even with rational expectations the economy may be 'stuck' at an undesirable equilibrium.

7.4 IMPLICATIONS FOR MACROECONOMIC POLICY

At this point a brief discussion of economic policy is irresistible. In earlier parts of the book several references have been made to several policy implications which have been drawn, usually rashly, from a job-search analysis. I shall focus attention on inflation and unemployment problems since these appear to be the main issues surrounding job-search theory and labour economics generally.

The crux of the issue is how best to achieve a low, stable inflation rate and low rates of unemployment. There are many shades of opinion on these issues, coloured largely by degrees of belief in the desirability of government involvement.

The UK now enjoys a relatively low and relatively stable inflation rate, though there is a feeling that the peace on this front is a fragile one. With evidence that the economy is undergoing some structural change any substantial increase in demand may prompt more of a price response (accompanied by increased imports) than a quantity response. On the other hand, it is clear from the discussion earlier that job-search theory does not provide unreserved support for the view that aggregate demand policies are necessarily ineffective in influencing unemployment in the long run. On the one hand, increased demand increases matching opportunities thus reducing friction. Moreover, by paying attention to the sectoral distribution of demand a government may, in principle, minimise the inflationary consequences of employment thus creating real output expansions. In terms of our earlier discussions, the government may manipulate the pattern of demand to induce the 'right' sort of change in the real wage distribution. To this extent the search theory finds it hard to attribute a role to government which does not involve the *allocation* of resources.

Of course, it is possible to deny any role for government in determining real outputs and there is a strong feeling that whatever the deficiencies of markets in producing an allocative efficient and high volume of output, governments on the whole do even worse! As always in these matters, pointing out the inefficiencies present in decentralised market economies does not, on its own, constitute an *a priori* case for government intervention. On the face of it, the information required by a government working to coordinate a particular sectoral distribution of demand is formidable.

If blanket fiscal policies are not condoned by search theory, the question remains as to the justification for some other much publicised unemployment-reducing measures. There appears to be two main alternatives. The first is to make unemployment more costly by reducing unemployment benefit. Jobs are taken up more quickly and unemployment caused by frictions reduced. Second is the use of market-directed policies to stimulate employment in particular sectors or regions.

The idea that unemployment will be reduced by cutting unemployment benefit or restricting entitlement is often justified by reference to job-search models. In fact, there is no basis in theory or on available evidence that unemployment would be significantly affected by these proposals. In particular the problem of long-term unemployment (durations in excess of twelve months) is unlikely to be affected at all by reductions in unemployment benefit. The reader is referred to section 6.4 for the theoretical reasons, and to section 5.3 for empirical evidence in support of this view.

So-called 'market-directed' programmes are usually discussed as an accompaniment to model-demand expansions. There is an acknowledgement that at least some workers are demand-constrained but that structural difficulties (decline of regions, industries and markets) make demand expansions alone of little value. Government-sponsored retraining programmes, relocation grants and a degree of manpower planning are thought necessary to assist in the otherwise sluggish response of labour markets to structural change.

The question of whether *permanent* reductions in inflation requires a role for incomes policy in order that monetary restraint is not accompanied by high unemployment could also be approached through a search theory of the labour market. To date, no complete treatment of the effects of incomes policies on job-search behaviour exists. Any views on this are necessarily speculative, but if wage movements are inhibited, greater quantity adjustments and possibly increased involuntary turnover are more likely. 'Distortions' of the wage-offer distribution produced by incomes policies may also lead to increased voluntary turnover and inefficient job break-ups.

7.5 CONCLUSION

This chapter has attempted to do little more than raise some quite general issues of macroeconomics in a job-search framework. None of the policy implications rests uniquely on a 'job-search' view of the world, but explicit recognition of the numerous dynamic paths possible, of multiple equilibria in search markets, and of externalities in matching processes casts doubt on the view that 'correct' macroeconomic policies are obvious or enduring.

Conclusion

The theoretical contribution of job-search analysis impinges on several of the traditional areas of economics. At its most general it forces us to think of market activity as a process involving decentralised and uncoordinated exchange between agents. The result of the process is a market outcome with properties quite different from those associated with static models. We can envisage a search equilibrium involving wage dispersion, turnover, unemployment and inefficiencies resulting from information and matching externalities.

At its most specific, the job-search theory gives us a variety of models of individual behaviour, enabling quite detailed studies of turnover, wage determination, unemployment benefit payments, job tenure and unemployment duration.

The empirical literature is only just showing signs of maturity resulting from both econometric developments and the increasing use of survey data. The potential here for serious study of labour market dynamics in practice is enormous.

A large amount of theoretical work on market equilibrium remains to be done, making much of the existing work tentative. For this reason, unguarded use of the theory for policy purposes would be rash. However, the indications are that search theory is unlikely to support macroeconomic policies of unfettered expansionism or of single-minded deflationism. Furthermore, job-search theory would seem to provide a role of microeconomic policies to accompany the broader aspects of economic managment. The allocation of resources and the level of economic activity are hard to distinguish and given the complexities of the workings of markets, policies aimed at controlling aggregate demand without regard to market adjustments are in serious danger of being counterproductive. Both Keynesian and monetarist policy-makers over the years have displayed an extraordinary naïvety in assuming that the workings within markets will produce an outcome consistent with the direction of macroeconomic policy.

Notes

CHAPTER 1

1. Another possibility requiring the searcher to have somewhat different information is that search takes place systematically. In this case the searcher knows enough to be able to rank firms in descending order of their wage offers. The searcher then visits each firm in turn to discover whether there is a vacancy. Salop (1973) has studied this type of job search problem and I return to it later.
2. The first application of this rule to the job-search problem is Stigler (1962).
3. It looks rather awkward because the choice variable n is an integer. For another treatment of this (in the context of a consumer search problem) see Hey (1979a), section 11.2.
4. A sequential search model which uses this decision rule is said to have the 'reservation wage property'. Not *all* sequential models do. In the Chapter 2 this property is *derived*; for the moment it is simply *assumed*.
5. Using (1.5) and (1.4) it can also be verified that $R(r^*) = r^*$, which suggests that the optimal reservation wage is such that the searcher is indifferent between continuing search (with return $R(r^*)$) and accepting exactly r^*.
6. For example, the searcher must be convinced that $F^*(W)$ is normal and is currently busy in updating prior beliefs about its mean and/or variance. As long as the underlying belief about $F^*(.)$ is correct then using Bayesian techniques to update information about distributional parameters can form part of an optimal policy. See DeGroot (1970) for details.
7. The issues raised briefly here, along with results of some experiments involving *ad hoc* rules, are to be found in Hey (1982).
8. For example Hey (1982) and Schotter and Braunstein (1981).

CHAPTER 2

1. The requirement that $V(\mathcal{W}) > 0$ is explained fully in section 2.4. Briefly it amounts to making search a worthwhile activity for the individual. More generally we would have $V(\mathcal{W}) > b$ where b is the per period return to the next best activity to search unemployment.
2. For our purposes it is immaterial whether the weak inequality applies to $w \geqq r$ or $w \leqq r$, as r is the marginal wage offer.
3. Again, the position of the weak inequality is not important. We could have $V(r^*) \leqq b$ and $V(r^*) > b$ (as written), or $V(r^*) < b$ and $V(r^*) \geqq b$.
4. The process may actually be a little more involved than this. Of course, as firms make wage-offer revisions 'on their way' (as it were) to the reservation wage the distribution $F(w)$ changes, thus inducing changes in the reservation wage by searchers. Hence the reservation wage, which finally constitutes the common wage offer, may well be different from the initial reservation wage which existed before wage-offer revision started. How far away the final wage offer is from the initial reservation wage depends on the size of wage adjustment made by firms, and the response in the reservation wage to changes in the wage-offer distribution.
5. Following Feinberg (1978b).

CHAPTER 3

1. Although the searcher could search forever, we know that because of the search cost the (expected) duration of search is finite.
2. Except r_1^* which is zero as long as $V_1^* > o$; that is, as long as search is *worth while* when just one period remains.
3. This method is outlined in the survey by Lippman and McCall (1976a) with the difference that 'offers' are defined as 'lifetime income' offers, with $G(.)$ being the distribution of lifetime incomes across firms. Redefining w appropriately, we have, instead of (3.20):

$$\tilde{V}_t^*(y) = \max \left\{ y, -c + \int_o^\infty \tilde{V}_{t-1}^*(x)dG(x) \right\} \tag{3.20}$$

and instead of (3.22):

$$y_t^* = -c + \int_o^\infty \tilde{V}_{t-1}^*(x)dG(x) \tag{3.22}$$

The basic result that y_t^* falls over time is preserved.

4. Of course, in an infinite horizon model, a wage lower than the reservation wage is *never* accepted. In the last period of a finite horizon model (with recall) it pays to take the best of previous offers however they stand in relation to the reservation wage used earlier.
5. Strictly speaking, it is a reservation income (utility) value as in note 3.
6. Few workers would find it necessary or desirable to become unemployed before finding another job. Most of us would prefer to have a job lined up before resigning!
7. The model is of the infinite horizon variety.
8. The (Arrow–Pratt) measure of absolute risk-aversion is defined as

$$R_A(M) \equiv -\frac{U''(M)}{U'(M)} \quad \text{all } M$$

If $R_A'(M) < o$ then the utility function $U(.)$ exhibits decreasing absolute risk-aversion (Hey, 1979b).
9. Instead of working in terms of the joint distribution of w and s, I choose to work in terms of the joint distribution of w and $w + s \ (=u)$. From the point of view of the general solution strategy the difference is immaterial.
10. To arrive at this sufficient condition, integrate (3.43) by parts and differentiate with respect to w. The condition is known as first-degree stochastic dominance. Distributions of U associated with higher wage offers stochastically dominate (in the first-degree) distribution associated with lower w-values.
11. This represents an expansion in the set of acceptable offers. In general, this will be the effect of an increase in search cost even when the model does not possess the reservation wage property.

CHAPTER 4

1. By dismissal I mean a permanent separation. A temporary separation, in which a worker is still attached to a firm though currently out of work, is commonly referred to as a lay-off. Circumstances under which mutually agreed (temporary) lay-offs feature in contracts are discussed in a large literature. Hart (1983) is a useful survey.
2. See for example Spence (1973).
3. Alternatively x is the marginal physical product and produce price is normalised at unity.

4. A few authors have touched on the possible connection between search and implicit contracts, for example, Burdett and Mortensen (1980) and Cothren (1983).
5. See Hoel (1971), p. 247.
6. The inverse of cosh (x) exists for $x > 1$ which in this case requires $b \geqslant \frac{1}{2}$. See Hardy (1963), p. 416.

CHAPTER 5

1. Often referred to as the 'replacement ratio'.
2. Stephenson (1976) has noted the important difference between the reservation wage concept of search theory and the 'asking wage' notion derived from sample surveys. Examples are not hard to find. For example, in Kasper (1967) the asking wage is the answer to the question: "What rate are you currently seeking?" This rate is found by Kasper to fall as unemployment continues.
3. Actually, the question asked by Feinberg is: "How much would a job have to pay for you to be willing to move?" The resulting evidence is therefore relevant for search models which allow moving costs (Hey and McKenna, 1979).
4. In addition to the three listed here, there are other models which would produce falling reservation wages: increasing search costs (Rice, 1978), wealth effects (Danforth, 1979) and change in the search environment (Lippman and McCall, 1976c). To my knowledge no empirical work on these specific hypotheses has been undertaken.
5. The existence of a unique reservation wage when the distribution of wage offers is unknown is not guaranteed in general. This was discussed in section 3.7.
6. The 'gain' is the value of the wage offer capitalised over six years.
7. In a survey of the unemployed, completed spells will be reported by those who have found work between the time they were selected for interview and the time of int... period of two or more weeks.
8. See Salant (1977) for the derivation of
9. If Var D is large (relative to $E^2[s]$) then .
10. The probability that unemployment end since $g(t)$ is (roughly) the probability th just t periods. Further, the probabilit ends during t, $t + dt$ *given* that unempl

before t is $g(t)dt/[1 - G(t)]$ which, of course, is exactly the interpretation of (5.5). Hence $p(t)dt = g(t)dt/[1 - G(t)]$. Integrating this over all points of time x from o to t gives $\int_o^t p(x)dx = -ln[1 - G(t)]$, $\mid$ dividing through by -1 and taking exponents gives the result (5.6) in the text.

11. Unless the researcher knows the correct joint distribution in the stock and in the flow. For example, the problem might appear simple if it is known that observables and unobservables are independently distributed in the flow, but this does not in general guarantee independence in the stock (Lancaster and Chesher, 1983).

12. The normalised version is (5.10) divided through by σ.

13. Ordinary least squares gives less efficient results.

14. Lancaster (1979), Nickell (1979), Lancaster and Nickell (1980).

15. This form of ψ_2 must still be simple enough to allow specifications of $p(t)$, $g(t)$ and (5.13).

16. $\psi_1 = v \exp \{x'\beta\}$

17. For the derivation of (5.22) see Lancaster and Chesher (1983).

CHAPTER 6

1. These results are neatly summarised by Danforth as indicating that (a) the rich are more choosy, (b) the rich search longer, and (c) the rich get richer. Proof of these findings and the full model specification are found in Danforth (1979).

2. See any recent labour economics text such as Addison and Siebert (1979), Chapter 3; Fleisher and Kniesner (1980), Chapter 4; and Joll *et al.* (1983), Chapters 1 and 2.

3. There is a slight complication in the behaviour of l between τ and $\tau + 1$. See Burdett (1979b), p. 169.

4. The individual 'chooses' p and w through the search process. In the comparative statics to follow these are treated as exogenous variables, in the sense that their *ex post* values are allowed to change.

5. Key features of this model were used also in Seater (1979) in a study of vacancy contacts.

6. In Seater's (1977) paper l, h and s are measured in hours per week so that $l(t) = 168 - h(t) - s(t)$.

7. The ambiguities represented by ? are not present for *all* t but may be signed differently in different phases.

8. An earlier paper by Whipple (1973) also considered consumption and job-search decisions, but is principally concerned with the effect of government programmes on unemployment. The effects of risk-aversion are not studied explicitly.

9. I use the term laid-off to mean either a permanent *or* a temporary involuntary separation.

10. Notice that if λ were uncertain at the time of job-acceptance, the analysis of section 3.6 would be appropriate. It appears to be an unnecessary complication to consider this possibility here.

11. That a reservation wage policy is optimal in this case is easily established.

12. This requires that a lay-off is correlated to an individual's productivity or reliability.

13. Except in the special case in which the previous wage rate is identical with the current reservation wage.

14. The behaviour of reservation wages over the cycle; that is, when the lay-off rate changes can be inferred from these studies. If benefits are not earnings-related, Hey and Mavromaras (1981) show that an improvement in the economic climate (a shifting to the left of the distribution of lay-off probabilities over firms) increases reservation wages. I return to macroeconomic inferences of this kind in the following chapter.

15. On the other hand, individuals with wealth and who are able to borrow (that is, where a perfect capital market is available) should receive zero unemployment benefit early in their unemployment spell, rising to a positive but constant amount, so long as they are unable to influence the probability of getting a job.

16. See the papers by Diamond (1982a) and Pissarides (1984).

CHAPTER 7

1. It is not my intention to set up a 'straw man'. The simple model described here has been the target of criticism by Okun (1981), Chapter 2, who appears to regard it as the main if not the only *job-search* interpretation of macrodynamics.

2. The ratio of each firm's wage offer to a general index of retail prices.

3. A full discussion of this subject may be found in Joll *et al.* (1983), Chapter 8.

4. I include here institutional constraints.

5. For a detailed discussion of some institutional considerations of pricing through the cycle, see Okun (1981), Chapter 4.

6. Usually referred to as its 'natural rate'. I avoid this usage here because it is often regarded as a fixed number, whereas the

correct interpretation is that it is a (determinate) *function* of various structural features of the economy's productivity. I refer to this again in the section on long-run adjustment.

7. This is as near as possible to saying that everybody is on their demand and supply curves.

8. Suppose all workers are risk-neutral, and that money wages adjust differentially, then the reservation wage distribution will shift to the right (left) if the distribution of real wage offers undergoes a mean preserving increase (decrease) in dispersion.

Appendices

A.1 DISCOUNTING

Consider a job which pays w per period. clearly a wage received immediately is worth exactly w, but what about the value now of wages received in future periods? Let i be an appropriate interest rate in the sense that if the period is a *week* then i is a *weekly* interest rate, and so on. Suppose we are offered a choice between an amount x_1 received immediately, or w received one period hence, then since x_1 could earn interest during the next period it would then have a value $x_1(1 + i)$. So, to be indifferent between x_1 received now and w received in one period's time we must have:

$$x_1(1 + i) = w$$

so that:

$$x_1 = \frac{w}{(1 + i)}$$

and x_1 is exactly the present value for w received one period hence.

By similar reasoning, an amount x_2 received immediately is only comparable with w received in two periods' time if (since $(1 + i)x_2$ could be reinvested for the second period):

$$x_2(1 + i) + i(1 + i)x_2 = w$$

or:

$$x_2 = \frac{w}{(1 + i)^2}$$

Hence, if w is paid in *each* of the following T periods the *total* present value of the stream of ws is:

$$PV_T = w + \frac{w}{(1 + i)} + \frac{w}{(1 + i)^2} + \ldots + \frac{w}{(1 + i)^T}$$

Before attempting to simplify this, consider the case where

151

$T \to \infty$, and define a discount factor (used in the text) as:

$$\varrho = \frac{1}{(1 + i)}$$

then:

$$PV_\infty = w \sum_{t=0}^{\infty} \varrho^t$$

but since $0 < \varrho < 1$:

$$\sum_{t=0}^{\infty} \varrho^t = \frac{1}{(1 - \varrho)}$$

and the total present value of w received in each period from now and forever is:

$$PV_\infty = \frac{w}{(1 - \varrho)}$$

As a simple extension to this, suppose w is received in all future periods but not in the current period, then the total present value is:

$$PV'_\infty = w \sum_{t=1}^{\infty} \varrho^t$$

$$= \varrho w \sum_{t=0}^{\infty} \varrho^t$$

$$= \frac{\varrho w}{(1 - \varrho)}$$

$$= \frac{w}{i}$$

As another extension, suppose w is received only for the following T periods, then the worker does not receive w from $T + 1$ onwards, and the total present value is:

$$PV_T = w \sum_{t=0}^{\infty} \varrho^t - w \sum_{t=T+1}^{\infty} \varrho^t$$

$$= w \frac{(1 - \varrho^{T+1})}{(1 - \varrho)}$$

A.2   CONDITIONAL EXPECTATION

I demonstrate here that for a random variable $(rv)X$ with distribution function $F(X)$ and $X \in (0, \infty)$, then:

$$\int_o^y X dF(X) = E[X \mid X \leqslant y] Pr[X \leqslant y] \qquad \text{for any } y \in (0, \infty)$$

or, since $Pr[X \leqslant y] = F(y)$:

$$\frac{\int_o^y X dF(X)}{F(y)} = E[X \mid X \leqslant y]$$

Let Z be the *rv* 'all values of X no greater than y' with distribution function $G(Z)$, then for any $x \leqslant y$:

$$Pr[Z \leqslant x] = \frac{Pr[X \leqslant x]}{Pr[X \leqslant y]}$$

$$G(x) = \frac{F(x)}{F(y)}$$

and so:

$$g(x) = \frac{f(x)}{F(y)}$$

Multiplying both sides by x and integrating over all $x \leqslant y$ gives:

$$\int_o^y X g(X) dX = \frac{\int_o^y X f(X) dX}{F(y)}$$

or, in the earlier notation:

$$\int_o^y X dG(X) = \frac{\int_o^y X dF(X)}{F(y)}$$

Now:

$$\int_o^y X dG(X) = E[Z]$$
$$= E[X \mid X \leqslant y]$$

hence:

$$\int_o^y X dF(X) = E[X \mid X \leqslant y] Pr[X \leqslant y]$$

A.3   INTEGRATION

(a)   Integration by parts

Consider two continuous functions $F(X)$ and $G(X)$ with derivatives $f(X)$ and $g(X)$, respectively. Clearly, the derivative of $F(X)G(X)$ is, by the product rule of differential:

$$\frac{d}{dX}(F(X)G(X)) = f(X)G(X) + F(X)g(X)$$

Integrating both sides gives:

$$F(X)G(X) = \int G(X)f(X)dX + \int F(X)g(X)dX$$
$$= \int G(X)dF(X) \quad + \int F(X)dG(X)$$

hence:

$$\int G(X)dF(X) = F(X)G(X) - \int F(X)dG(X)$$

(b)   Consider the integral

$$G(x) = \int_{v(x)}^{u(x)} f(x, Y)dY$$

then:

$$G'(x) = \int_{v(x)}^{u(x)} df(x, Y)dY - v'(x)f(x, v(x)) + u'(x)f(x, u(x))$$

References

Addison, J. T. and Siebert, W. S. (1979), *The Market for Labor: An Analytical Treatment*, Goodyear, Santa Monica.

Ameniya, T. (1984), 'Tobit models: a survey', *Journal of Econometrics*, 24(1/2). Annals 3–61.

Arrow, K. J. (1959), 'Toward a theory of price adjustment', in Abramovitz, M., *et al.*, *The Allocation of Economic Resources*, Stanford University Press, Stanford, pp. 41–51.

Atkinson, A. B., Gomulka, J., Mickelwright, J. and Rau, N. (1984), 'Unemployment benefit, duration and incentives in Britain: How robust is the evidence?' *Journal of Public Economics*, 23(1/2), February/March, 3–26.

Axell, B (1974), 'Price dispersion and information — an adaptive sequential search model', *Swedish Journal of Economics*, 76(1), March 77–98.

Axell, B. (1977), 'Search market equilibrium', *Scandinavian Journal of Economics*, 79(1), March, 20–40.

Axelsson, R., and Löfgren, K. G. (1977), 'The demand for labour and search activity in the Swedish labour market', *European Economic Review*, 9(3), August, 345–60.

Azariadis, C. (1975), 'Implicit contracts and underemployment equilibria', *Journal of Political Economy*, 83(6), December 1183–202.

Baily, M. N. (1977), 'On the theory of lay-offs and unemployment', *Econometrica*, 45(5), July, 1043–64.

Barnes, W. F. (1975), 'Job search models, the duration of unemployment and the asking wage: some empirical evidence', *Journal of Human Resources*, 10(2), Spring, 230–40.

Barron, J. M. (1975), 'Search in the labor market and the duration of unemployment: some empirical evidence', *American Economic Review*, 65(5), December, 934–42.

Barron, J. M. and Gilley, O. W. (1981), 'Job search and vacancy contacts', *American Economic Review*, 71(4), September, 747–52.

Barron, J. M. and McCafferty, S. (1977), 'Job search, labor supply and the quit decision: theory and evidence', *American Economic Review*, 67(4), September, 683–91.

Begg, D. (1982), *The Rational Expectations Revolution in Macroeconomics*, Philip Allan, Oxford.

Benhabib, J. and Bull, C. (1983), 'Job search: the choice of intensity', *Journal of Political Economy*, 91(5), October, 747–64.

Black, M. (1980), 'Pecuniary implications of on-the-job search and quit activity', *Review of Economics and Statistics*, 62(2), May, 222–9.

Borjas, G. N. and Goldberg, M. S. (1978), 'The economics of job search: a comment, *Economic Inquiry*, 16(1), January, 119–25.

Bradshaw, T. F. and Scholl, J. L. (1976), 'The extent of job search during layoff', *Brookings Papers on Economic Activity*, 2, 515–24.

Burdett, K. (1977), 'On-the-job search and quit rates', in Artis, M and Nobay, A. R., *Studies in Modern Analysis*, Basil Blackwell, Oxford, pp. 23–53.

Burdett, K, (1978), 'A theory of employee search and quit rates', *American Economic Review*, 68(1), March, 212–20.

Burdett, K. (1979a), 'Unemployment insurance payments as a search subsidy', *Economic Inquiry*, 17 July, 333–43.

Burdett, K. 'Search, leisure and individual labor supply', in Lippman, S. A. and McCall, J. J. (eds), *op. cit.*, pp. 157–70.

Burdett, K. and Judd, K. L. (1983), 'Equilibrium price dispersion', *Econometrica*, 51(4), July, 955–69.

Burdett, K. and Mortensen, D. T. (1980), 'Search, layoffs and market equilibrium', *Journal of Political Economy*, 88(4), 652–72.

Butters, G. R. (1977), 'Equilibrium distributions of sales and advertising prices', *Review of Economic Studies*, 44(3), October, 465–92.

Carlson, J. A. and McAfee, R. P. (1983), 'Discrete equilibrium price dispersion', *Journal of Political Economy*, 91(3), June, 480–93.

Chapin, G. (1971), 'Unemployment insurance, job search and the demand for leisure', *Western Economic Journal*, 9(1), March, 102–7.

Chesher, A. and Lancaster, T. (1983), 'The estimation of models of labour market behaviour', *Review of Economic Studies*, 50(4), 163, October, 609–24.

Classen, K. P. (1979), 'Unemployment insurance and job search', in Lippman, S. A. and McCall, J. J. (eds), *op. cit.*, pp. 191–219.

Cothren, R. (1983), 'Job search and implicit contracts', *Journal of Political Economy*, 91(3), June, 494–504.

Danforth, J. P. (1979), 'On the role of consumption and decreasing absolute risk-aversion in the theory of job search', in Lippman, S. A. and McCall, J. J. (eds), *op. cit.*, pp. 109–31.

Degroot, M. N. (1970), *Optimal Statistical Decisions*, McGraw-Hill, New York.

Diamond, P. A. (1971), 'A model of price adjustment', *Journal of Economic Theory*, 3(2), 156–68.

Diamond, P. A. (1981), 'Mobility costs, frictional unemployment and efficiency', *Journal of Political Economy*, 89, 798–812.

Diamond, P. A. (1982a), 'Wage determination and efficiency in search equilibrium', *Review of Economic Studies*, 49(2), 156, April, 217–27.

Diamond, P. A. (1982b), 'Aggregate demand managment in search equilibrium', *Journal of Political Economy*, 90(5), October, 881–94.

Diamond, P. A. (1984), 'Money in search equilibrium', *Econometrica*, 52(1), January, 1–20.

Eaton, C. B. and Neher, P. A. (1975) 'Unemployment and optimal job search', *Journal of Political Economy*, 83(2), April, 355–75.

Eaton, C. B. and Watts, M. (1977), 'Wage dispersion, job vacancies and job search in equilibrium', *Economica*, 44(173), February, 23–35.

Ehrenberg, R. G. and Oaxaca, R. (1976), 'Unemployment insurance duration of unemployment and subsequent wage gain', *American Economic Review*, 66(5), December, 754–66.

Feinberg, R. M. (1975), 'Job search, minimum wages and labor force participation', *Journal of Economic Studies*, 2(2), November, 131–8.

Feinberg, R. M. (1977a), 'Search in the labor market and the duration of unemployment', *American Economic Review*, 67(5), December, 1011–13.

Feinberg, R. M. (1977b), 'Risk-aversion, risk and the duration of unemployment', *Review of Economics and Statistics*, 59(3), August, 264–71.

Feinberg, R. M. (1978a), 'The forerunner of the job search theory', *Economy Inquiry*, 16(1), January, 126–32.

Feinberg, R. M. (1978b), 'On the empirical importance of the job search theory', *Southern Economic Journal*, 45(2), October, 508–21.

Feinberg, R. M. (1978c), 'Labour force participation and the job search theory: tests of some neglected implications', *Journal of Economic Studies*, 5(1), May, 50–63.

Feinberg, R. M. and Johnson, W. R. (1977), 'The superiority of

158   *Uncertainty and the Labour Market*

sequential search: a calculation', *Southern Economic Journal*, 43(4), April, 1594–8.

Feldstein, M. and Poterba, J. (1984), 'Unemployment insurance and reservation wages', *Journal of Public Economics*, 23(1/2), February/March, 141–67.

Fisher, F. M. (1970), 'Quasi-competitive price adjustment by individual firms: a preliminary paper', *Journal of Economic Theory*, 2(3), June, 195–206.

Fisher, F. M. (1972), 'On price adjustment without an auctioneer', *Review of Economic Studies*, 29, January, 1–15.

Fisher, F. M. (1973), 'Stability and competitive equilibrium in two models of search and individual price adjustment', *Journal of Economic Theory*, 6(5), October, 446–70.

Fleisher, B. M. and Kniesner, T. J. (1980), *Labor Economics*, Prentice-Hall, N.J. (2nd edn).

Flemming, J. S. (1978), 'Aspects of optimal unemployment insurance; search leisure, saving and capital market imperfections', *Journal of Public Economics*, 10(3), December, 403–25.

Friedman, M. (1968), 'The role of monetory policy', *American Economic Review*, 58, 1–17.

Gal, S., Lansberger, M. and Levykson, P. (1981), 'A compound strategy for search in the labor market', *International Economic Review*, 22(3), October, 597–608.

Gastwirth, J. L. (1976), 'On probabilistic models of consumer search for information', *Quarterly Journal of Economics*, 90(1), February, 38–50.

Gayer, P. and Goldfarb, R. S. (1972), 'Job search, the duration of unemployment and the Phillips curve; comment', *American Economic Review*, 62(4), September, 714–17.

Gronau, R. (1971), 'Information and frictional unemployment', *American Economic Review*, 61(2), May, 290–301.

Grossman, H. I. (1973), 'Aggregate demand, job search and employment', *Journal of Political Economy*, 81(6), November, 1353–67.

Hahn, F. H. (1982), *Money and Inflation*, Basil Blackwell, Oxford.

Hall, J. R., Lippman, S. A. and McCall, J. J. (1979), 'Expected utility-maximizing job search' in Lippman, S. A. and McCall, J. J. (eds), *op. cit.*, pp. 133–55.

Hardy, G. H. (1963), *Pure Mathematics*, Cambridge University Press, Cambridge (10th edn).

Hart, O. D. (1983), 'Optimal labour contracts under asymmetric information: an introduction', *Review of Economic Studies*, 50, 3–35.

Heckman, J. and Singer, B. (1984a), 'A method for minimizing the impact of distribution assumptions in econometric models of duration data', *Econometrica*, 52(2), March, 271–320.

Heckman, J. and Singer, B. (1984b), 'The identifiability of the proportional hazards model', *Review of Economic Studies*, 51(2), 165, April.

Heckman, J. and Singer, B. (1984c), 'Econometric duration analysis', *Journal of Econometrics*, 24(1/2), Annals 63–132.

Hey, J. D. (1974), 'Price adjustment in an atomistic market', *Journal of Economic Theory*, 8(4), August, 483–99.

Hey, J. D. (1977), 'On-the-job search and quit rates: discussion' in Artis, M. and Nobay, A. R. (eds), *Studies in Modern Economic Analysis*, Basil Blackwell, Oxford, pp. 45–57.

Hey, J. D. (1979a), *Uncertainty in Microeconomics*, Martin Robertson, Oxford.

Hey, J. D. (1979b), 'A simple generalised stopping rule', *Economics Letters*, 2, 115–20.

Hey, J. D. (1981), *Economics in Disequilibrium*. Martin Robertson, Oxford.

Hey, J. D. (1982), 'Search for rules for search', *Journal of Economic Behaviour and Organisation*, 3, 65–81.

Hey, J. D. and Mavromaras, K. G. (1981), 'The effect of unemployment insurance on the riskiness of occupational choice', *Journal of Public Economics*, 16, 317–41.

Hey, J. D. and McKenna, C. J. (1979), 'To move or not to move?', *Economica*, 46(182), May, 175–85.

Hoel, P. G. (1971), *Introduction to Mathematical Statistics*, Wiley, London. (4th edn).

Holen, A. (1977), 'Effects of unemployment insurance entitlement on duration of job search', *Industrial and Labor Relations Review*, 30(4), July, 445–50.

Holtman, A. G. (1969), 'Teacher salaries and the economic benefit of search', *Journal of Human Resources*, 4(1), Winter, 99–102.

Hvidding, J. M. (1979), 'Speculative behavior, search and waiting: a note on a potential ambiguity in the interpretation of job search model', *Southern Economic Journal*, 45(4), April, 1248–53.

Ionnides, Y. M. (1975), 'Market allocation through search equilibrium adjustment and price dispersion', *Journal of Economic Theory*, 11, 247–62.

Joll, C., McKenna, C. J., McNabb, R. and Shorey, J. (1983), *Developments in Labour Market Analysis*, George Allen & Unwin, London.

Jovanovic, B. (1984), 'Matching, turnover and unemployment', *Journal of Political Economy*, 92(1), February, 108–22.

160 *Uncertainty and the Labour Market*

Kahn. L. M. (1978), 'The return to job search: a test of two models', *Review of Economics and Statistics*, 60(4), November, 496–503.

Karni, E. and Schwartz, A. (1977), 'Search theory: the case of search with uncertain recall', *Journal of Economic Theory*, 16(1), October, 38–52.

Kasper, H. (1967), 'The asking price of labor and the duration of unemployment', *Review of Economics and Statistics*, 49(2), May, 165–72.

Kesselman, J. R. (1976), 'Tax effects on job search, training and work effort', *Journal of Public Economics*, 6(3), October, 255–72.

Kiefer, N. M. and Neumann, G. R. (1979a), 'An empirical job search model with a test of the constant reservation wage hypothesis', *Journal of Political Economy*, 87(1), February, 89–107.

Kiefer, N. M. and Neumann, G. R. (1979b), 'Estimation of wage offer distributions and reservation wages', in Lippman, S. A. and McCall, J. J. (eds), *op. cit.*

Kiefer, N. M. and Neumann, G. R. (1981), 'Individual effects in a non-linear model: explicit treatment of heterogeneity in the empirical job search model', *Econometrica*, 49(4), July 965–79.

Kohn, M. G. and Shavell, S. (1974), 'The theory of search', *Journal of Economic Theory*, 9(2), October, 93–123.

Lancaster, T. (1979), 'Econometric methods for the duration of unemployment', *Econometrica*, 47(4), July, 939–56.

Lancaster, T. and Chesher, A. (1983), 'An econometric analysis of reservation wage', *Econometrica*, 51(6), November, 1661–76.

Lancaster, T. and Nickell, S. (1980), 'The analysis of re-employment probabilities for the unemployed', *Journal of the Royal Statistical Society* (A), 143(2), 141–65.

Landsberger, M. and Peled, D. (1971), 'Duration of offers, price structure and the gain from search', *Journal of Economic Theory*, 16(2), October, 17–37.

Lippman, S. A. and McCall, J. J. (1976a), 'The economics of job search: a survey I', *Economic Inquiry*, 14(2), June, 155–89.

Lippman, S. A. and McCall, J. J. (1976b), 'The economics of job search: a survey II', *Economic Inquiry*, 14(3), September, 347–68.

Lippman, S. A. and McCall, J. J. (1976c), 'Job search in a dynamic economy', *Journal of Economic theory*, 12(3), 365–70.

Lippman, S. A. and McCall, J. J. (eds) (1979), *Studies in the Economics of Search*, North-Holland, Amsterdam.

Lippman, S. A. and McCall, J. J. (1980), 'Search unemployment:

mismatches, layoffs and unemployment insurance', *Scandinavian Journal of Economics*, 82(2), July, 253–72.
Lippman, S. A. and McCall, J. J. (1981), 'Progressive taxation in sequential decision-making'. *Journal of Public Economics*, 10, 35–52.
Lucas, R. E. and Prescott, E. C. (1974), 'Equilibrium search and unemployment', *Journal of Economic Theory*, 7(2), February, 188–209.
Lynch, L. M. (1983), 'Job search and youth unemployment', *Oxford Economic Papers*, 35 (Suppl.), November, 271–83.
McCafferty, S. (1978), 'A theory of semi-permanent wage search', *Southern Economic Journal*, 45(1), July, 46–62.
McCafferty, S. (1979), 'Wage dispersion and job search behaviour', *Journal of Economics and Business*, 31(3), Spring, 213–17.
McCafferty, S. (1980), 'Vacancies, discouraged workers and labour market dynamics', *Southern Economic Journal*, 47(1), July, 21–9.
McCall, J. J. (1965), 'The economics of information and optimal stopping rules', *Journal of Business*, 38(3), July, 300–17.
McCall, J. J. (1970), 'Economics of information and job search', *Quarterly Journal of Economics*, 84(1), February, 113–26.
McCall, J. J. (1972), 'Economics of information and job search: reply', *Quarterly Journal of Economics*, 86(1), February, 132–4.
McKenna, C. J. (1979), 'A solution to a class of sequential decision problems', *Economics Letters*, 3, 115–18.
McKenna, C. J. (1980), 'Wage offers, lay-offs and the firm in an uncertain labour market', *Manchester School*, 48(3), September, 255–64.
MacMinn, R. D. (1980a), 'Search and market equilibrium', *Journal of Political Economy*, 88(2), April, 308–27.
MacMinn, R. D. (1980b), 'Job search and the labor dropout problem reconsidered', *Quarterly Journal of Economics*, 95, August, 69–87.
Marston, S. T. (1975), 'The impact of unemployment insurance on job search', *Brookings Papers and Economic Activity*, 1, 13–48.
Mattila, J. P. (1974), 'Job-quitting and frictional unemployment', *American Economic Review*, 64(1), March, 235–9.
Mayhew, K. (1977), 'Earnings dispersion in local labour markets: implications for search behaviour', *Oxford Bulletin of Economics and Statistics*, 39(2), May, 93–107.
Mellow, W. (1978), 'Search costs and the duration of unemployment', *Economic Inquiry*, 16(2), July, 423–30.
Melnik, A. and Saks, D. H. (1977), 'Information and adaptive

162   *Uncertainty and the Labour Market*

search behavior: an empirical analysis', in Ashenfelter, O. and Oates, W. E. (eds), *Essays in Labor Market Analysis*, Wiley, New York.

Metcalf, D. (1973), 'Pay dispersion, information and returns to search in a professional labour market', *Review of Economic Studies*, 40(4), October, 491–506.

Mirman, L. J. and Porter, W. R. (1977), 'A microeconomic model of the labour market under uncertainty', *Economic Inquiry*, 12(2), June, 135–45.

Morgan, P. (1983), 'Search and optimal sample size', *Review of Economic Studies*, 50(4), October, 659–75.

Mortensen, D. T. (1970), 'Job search, the duration of unemployment and the Phillips curve', *American Economic Review*, 60(5), December, 847–62.

Mortensen, D. T. (1977), 'Unemployment insurance and job search decisions', *Industrial and Labor Relations Review*, 30(4), July, 505–17.

Nickell, S. J. (1979), 'Estimating the probability of leaving unemployment', *Econometrica*, 47(5), September, 1249–66.

Okun, A. (1981), *Prices and Quantities: A Macroeconomic Analysis*, Basil Blackwell, Oxford.

Parsons, D. O. (1973), 'Quit rates over time; a search and information approach', *American Economic Review*, 63(3), June, 340–401.

Parsons, D. O. (1977), 'Models of labor market turnover: a theoretical and empirical survey', in Ehrenberg, R. G. (ed.), *Research in Labor Economics*, vol. 1, pp. 185–223.

Peterson, R. L. (1972), 'Economics of information and job search: another view', *Quarterly Journal of Economics*, 86(1), February, 127–31.

Phelps, E. S. (1967), 'Phillips curves, expectations of inflation and optimal unemployment over time', *Economcia*, 34, 254–81.

Phelps, E. S. *et al.* (1970), *Microeconomics of Employment and Inflation Theory*, Macmillan, London.

Pissarides, C. A. (1974), 'Risk, job search and income distribution', *Journal of Political Economy*, 82, November, 1255–67.

Pissarides, C. A. (1976a), *Labour Market Adjustment*, Cambridge University Press, Cambridge.

Pissarides, C. A. (1976b), 'Job search and participation', *Economica*, 43(169), February, 33–49.

Pissarides, C. A. (1979), 'Equilibrium vacancies and unemployment in a model of employment agencies and random search', *Economics Journal*, 89(336), December, 818–33.

Pissarides, C. A. (1982), 'Job search and the duration of layoff unemployment', *Quarterly Journal of Economics*, 97(4), November, 543–67.

Pissarides, C. A. (1984), 'Efficient job rejection', *Economic Journal*, 94 (Suppl.), 97–108.

Reid, G. L. (1972), 'Job search and the effectiveness of job finding methods', *Industrial and Labour Relations Review*, 25(4), July, 479–95.

Reinganum, J. F. (1979), 'A simple model of equilibrium price dispersion', *Journal of Political Economy*, 87(4), August, 851–8.

Rice, P. (1978), 'Optimal search behaviour in a model with increasing costs', *Economics Letters*, 1(3), 211–15.

Rothschild, M. (1973), 'Models of market organisation with imperfect information: a survey, *Journal of Political Economy*, 81(6), 1283–1368.

Rothschild, M. (1974), 'Searching for the lowest price when the distribution of prices is unknown', *Journal of Political Economy*, 82(4), November, 689–712.

Salant, W. (1977), 'Search theory and duration data: a theory of sorts', *Quarterly Journal of Economics*, 91(1), February, 39–48.

Salop, S. C. (1973), 'Systematic job search and unemployment', *Review of Economics Studies*, 40(2), March, 191–202.

Salop, S. C. and Stiglitz, J. E. (1977), 'Bargains and ripoffs: a model of monopolistically competitive price dispersion', *Review of Economics Studies*, 44(3), October, 493–510.

Sant, D. T. (1977), 'Reservation wage rules and learning behaviour', *Review of Economics and Statistics*, 59(1), February, 43–9.

Schotter, A and Braunstein, Y. M. (1980), 'Economic search: an experimental study', *Economics Inquiry*, 19(1), June, 1–25.

Seater, J. J. (1977), 'A unified model of consumption, labor supply and job search', *Journal of Economics Theory*, 14(2), April, 349–72.

Seater, J. J. (1979), 'Job search and vacancy contacts', *American Economics Review*, 69(3), June, 411–22.

Shavell, S. and Weiss, L. (1979), 'The optimal payment of insurance benefit over time', *Journal of Political Economy*, 87(6), December, 1347–62.

Siven, C.-H. (1974), 'Consumption, supply of labor and search activity in an intertemporal perspective', *Swedish Journal of Economics*, 76(1), 44–61.

Spence, M. (1973), 'Job market signalling,' *Quarterly Journal of Economics*, 87(3), August, 355–74.

Stephenson, S. P. (1976), 'The economics of youth job search

164	*Uncertainty and the Labour Market*

behaviour', *Review of Economics and Statistics*, 58(1), February, 104–11.

Stigler, G. J. (1961), 'The economics of information', *Journal of Political Economy*, 69(3), June, 213–25.

Stigler, G. J. (1962), 'Information in the labor market', *Journal of Political Economy*, 70(5), October, S94–S105.

Watts, M. (1978), 'Screening, inter-firm exploitation and job search', *Scottish Journal of Political Economy*, 25(2), June 187–200.

Weintraub, E. R. (1977), 'The microfoundations of macro-economics', *Journal of Economic Literature*, 15(1), March, 1–23.

Whipple, D. (1973), 'A generalized theory of job search', *Journal of Political Economy*, 81(5), September, 1170–88.

Wilde, L. L. (1977), 'Labor market equilibrium under non-sequential search', *Journal of Economic Theory*, 16(2), December, 373–93.

Wilde, L. L. (1979), 'An information — theoretic apporach to job quits' in Lippman, S. A. and McCall, J. J. (eds) *op. cit.*

Index